AF505463

ACQUISITIONS:
THE FIRST DECADE
1977-1986

YALE CENTER FOR BRITISH ART
NEW HAVEN, CONNECTICUT, 1986

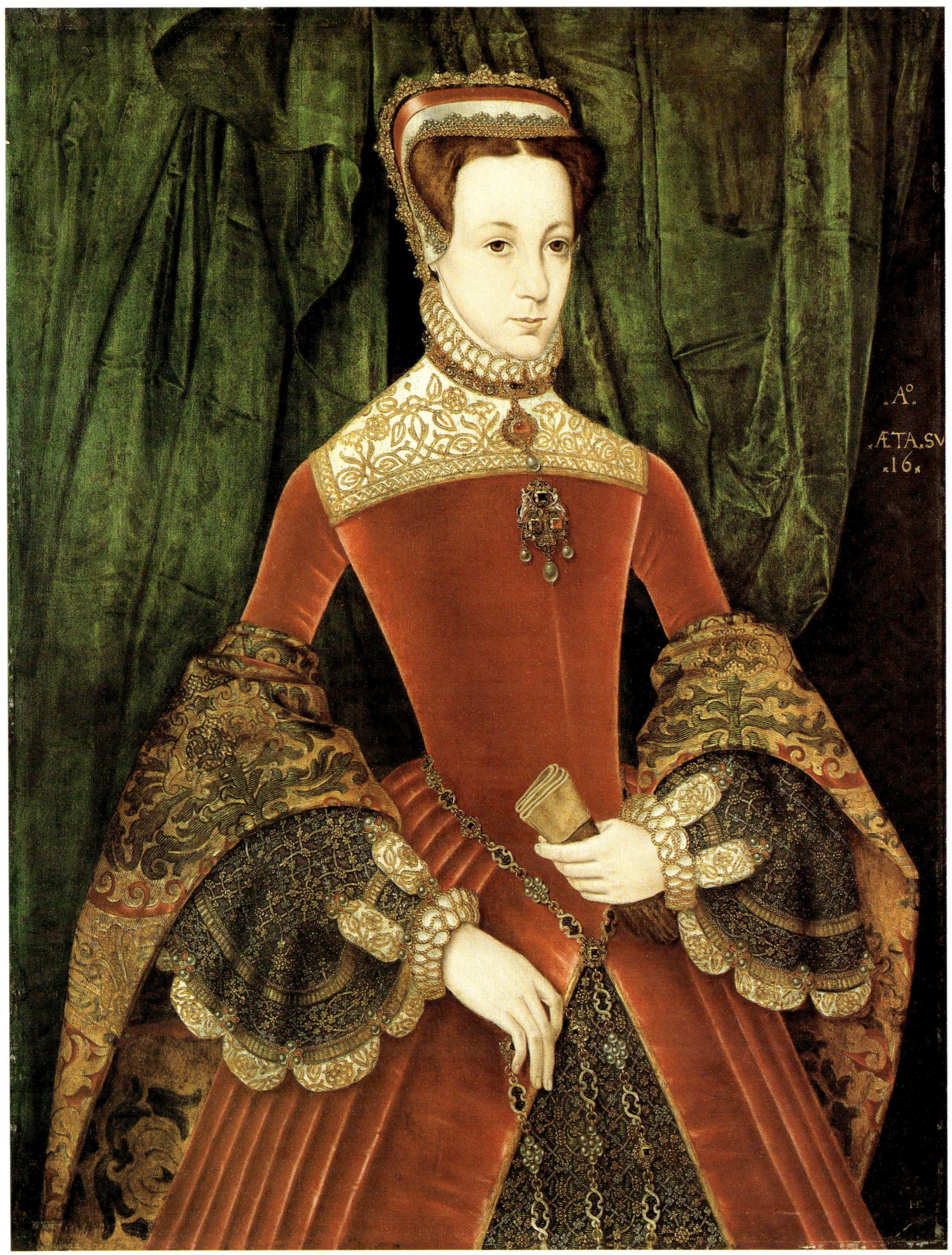

1. Hans Eworth, *Portrait of a Woman, possibly Mary Fitzalan, Duchess of Norfolk*, CAT. 15

INTRODUCTION

On Saturday, 23rd April 1977, *The Times* of London hailed 'a new era in Anglo-American cultural relations. On Tuesday [19th April] the Yale Center for British Art was opened to the public, which henceforth has free access to what is beyond question the finest collection of British oil paintings, watercolours, drawings, prints and illustrated books ever formed by a private individual.' By then, the reputation of the Paul Mellon Collection of British Art was established. At the inauguration of the Center ten years ago, Mr Mellon referred with too much modesty to 'the fruits of my amateur husbandry, this sturdy British tree with all its green branches.' The metaphor was chosen with care, and with the future in mind. The collection, like the Center itself, is alive and growing. After a decade of careful cultivation it displays new limbs as well as denser foliage upon some of the older ones. I refer, of course, both to the expansion of the collection into new areas such as the twentieth century, and to the acquisition of important works by artists already well represented: William Hogarth, Thomas Gainsborough, John Constable and J.M.W. Turner, to instance but four of the more obvious names.

In celebrating the expansion of the collections during the last ten years, our first debt is to our donors. Once again, Mr Mellon takes pride of place, both for the works of art he has given since the Center opened and for the funds he has made regularly available to our curatorial departments. Ever responsive to our needs, he has joined us with all of his sportsman's relish in pursuit of many a prize. Happily, his enthusiasm is infectious. The number of donors grows steadily with each year, as collectors respond to the appeal of the Center and recognise its importance as a repository for British art and archives. To those new friends, whose support is vital to the future of the institution, the exhibition pays tribute.

It also dares to look forward, in an attempt to stimulate fresh support for areas in which our holdings are either weak or non-existent. It could be argued that in our recent concentration upon late nineteenth- and early twentieth-century art we have neglected the period 1850-80. If so, we shall remedy the situation only if we are successful in appealing to some of those collectors whose enthusiasm for the Victorian era accounts for its current vogue. The exhibition earlier this year of Fay Godwin's *Land* served to highlight the absence of photography from the collections, in spite of the fact that it has been an important medium in British art for more than a century. Two examples suffice to illustrate present needs, and to advertise them.

Temporary exhibitions have indeed resulted in acquisitions. From the loans to *Eight Figurative Painters* (1981-82) we received as a gift the portrait drawing of *Christopher Dark* by Frank Auerbach (b.1931), and from *Stephen Buckley: Paintings 1969-1985*, *Concluding 8*. In anticipation of the *Sir David Wilkie* exhibition, which is scheduled to open early next year, we have been able to purchase a late self-portrait and an early and dazzling panel painting of *The Pedlar*. Incidentally, neither of these, nor the handsome drawing of *Captain Leigh and His Dragoman*, which we purchased in 1982, appears in this selection; all three are reserved for the monographic show which begins on 21st January 1987.

I must emphasise that the checklists which follow detail only those acquisitions which have been chosen, with care and some difficulty, to exhibit the range and quality of a decade of institutional collecting. They are selected from more than 35,000 objects accessioned since January 1977. At the opening, Mr Mellon ended his remarks by 'turning to the new Director, Ted Pillsbury, and his able staff,' professing for them 'nothing but confidence and admiration.' Both Malcolm Cormack and Joan Friedman have served throughout the past ten years as Curators of Paintings and Rare Books respectively. Andrew Wilton was the first Curator of Prints and Drawings with Patrick Noon, Curator since 1981, as his Assistant. To their efforts have been added those of Assistant Curators Susan Casteras (Paintings) and Scott Wilcox (Prints and Drawings) and Catalogue Librarian Elisabeth Fairman. In London the Center benefited originally from the expert advice of the late Sir Ellis Waterhouse and his successor as Director of Studies at the Paul Mellon Centre there, Dr Christopher White. Today Professor Michael Kitson and Dr Brian Allen maintain the tradition. The exhibition affords an opportunity to reflect on success and to celebrate, and above all to thank those who have contributed in different ways to the spectacular growth of this hardy British perennial in American soil.

DUNCAN ROBINSON
Director

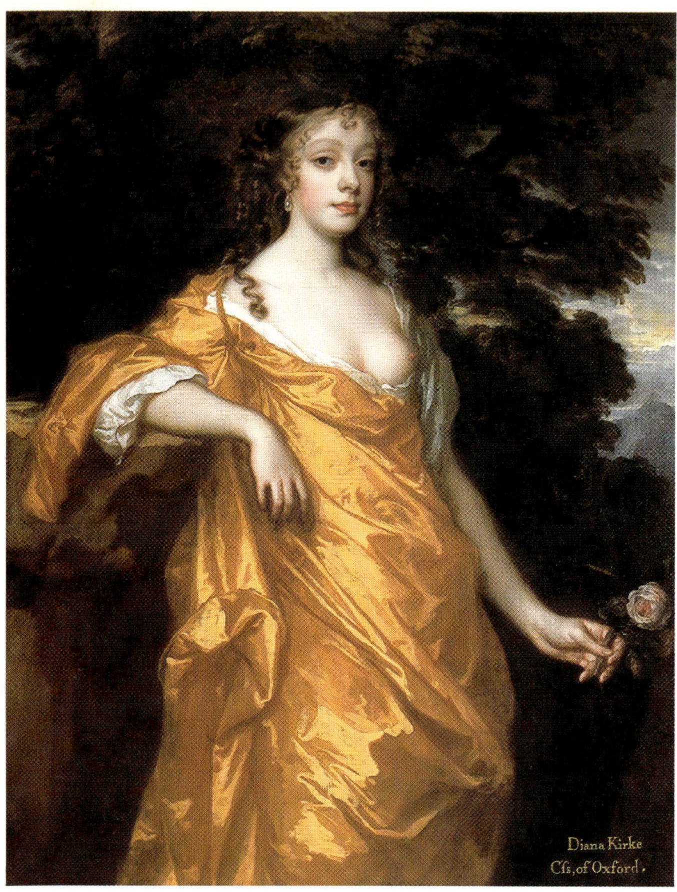

2. Sir Peter Lely, *Diana Kirke, later Countess of Oxford*, CAT. 35

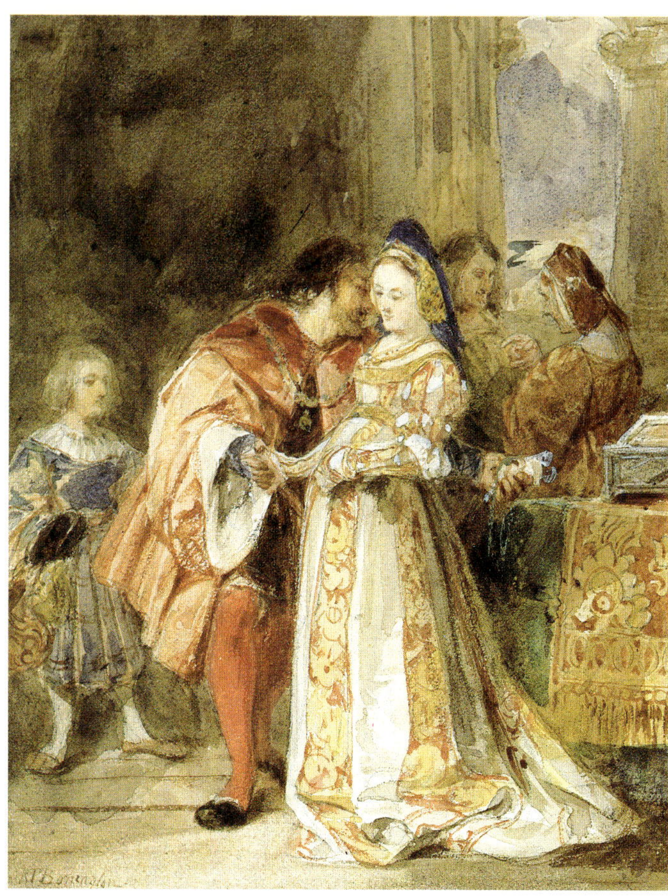

3. Richard Parkes Bonington, *The Present*, CAT. 73

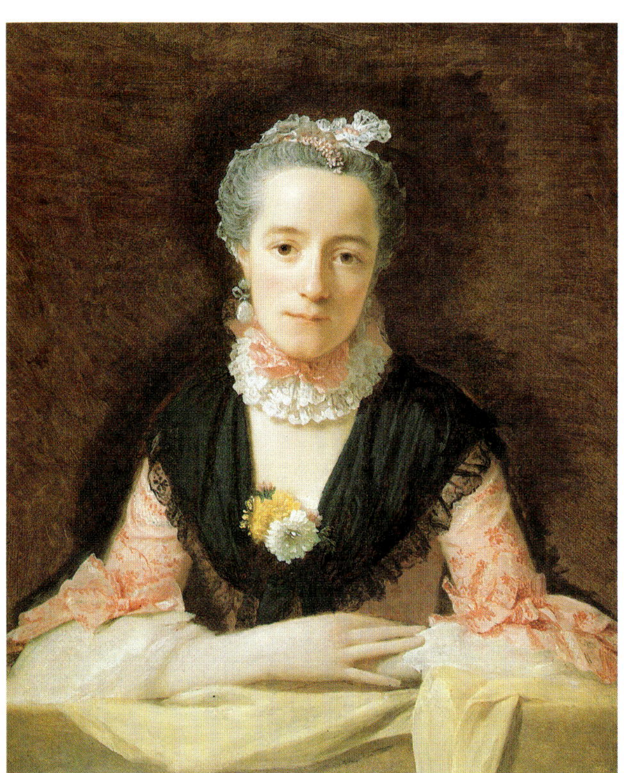

4. Allan Ramsay, *An Unknown Woman in a Pink Dress*, CAT. 44

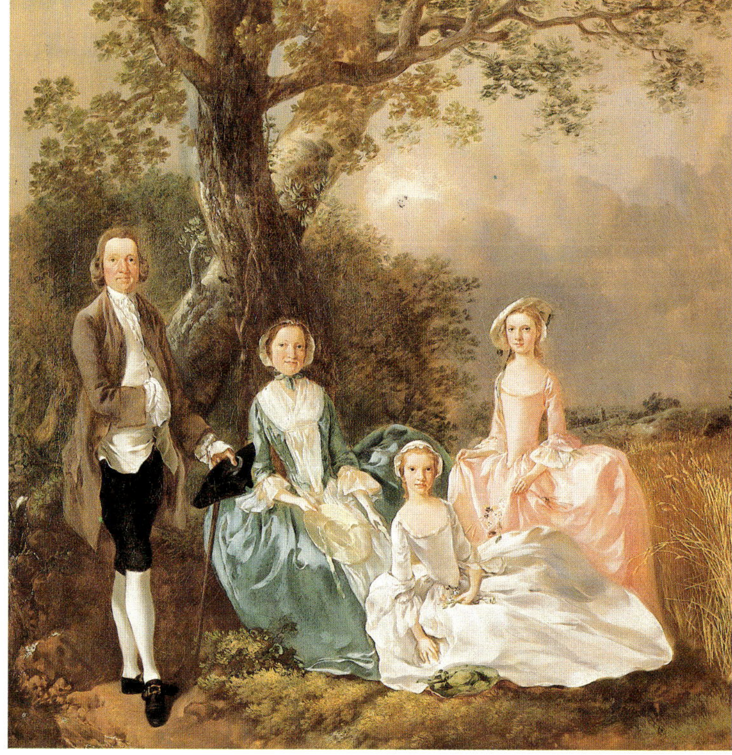

5. Thomas Gainsborough, R.A., *Mr. and Mrs. John Gravenor and their Daughters, Elizabeth and Dorothea*, CAT. 16

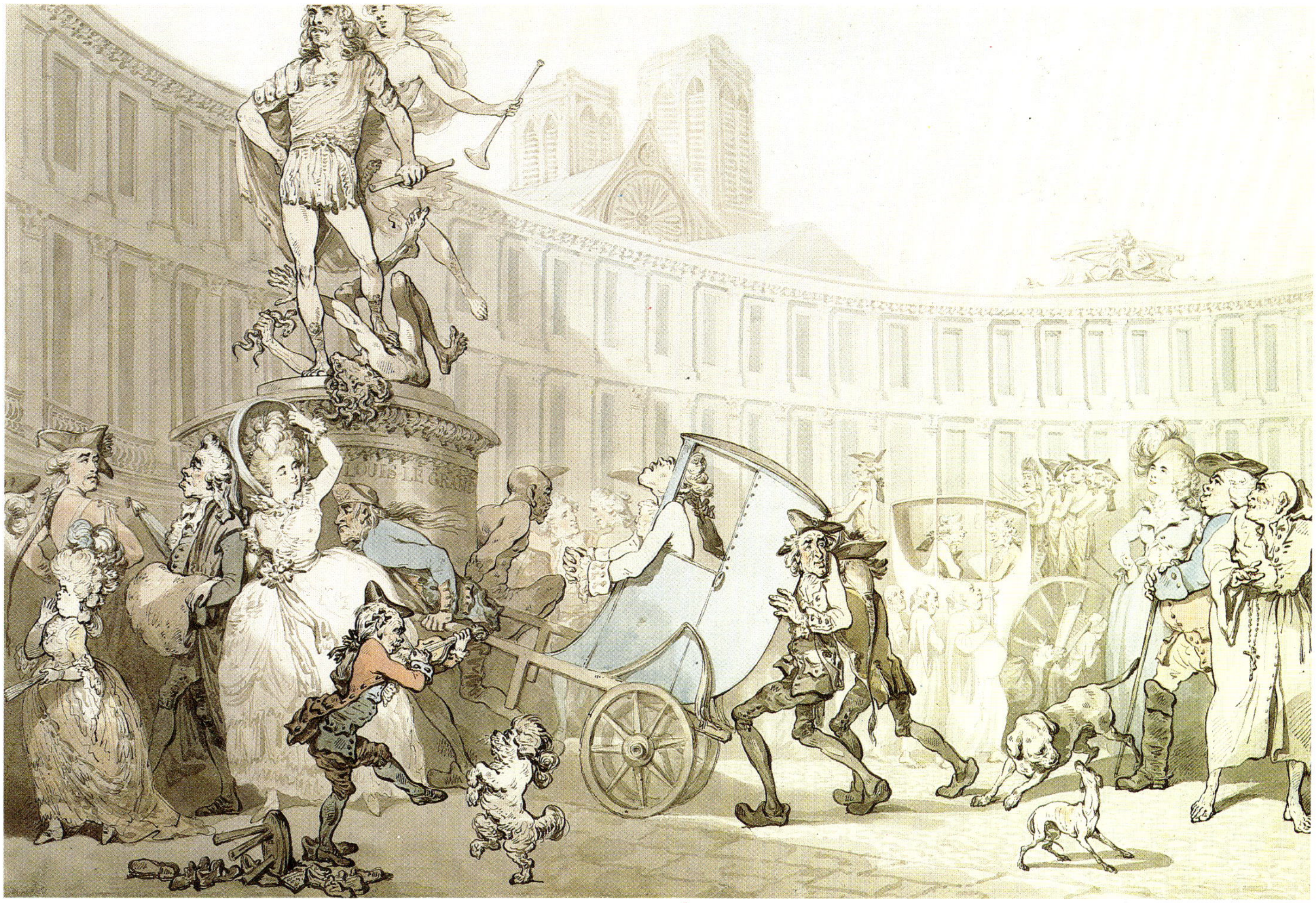

6. Thomas Rowlandson, *Place des Victoires*, CAT. 118

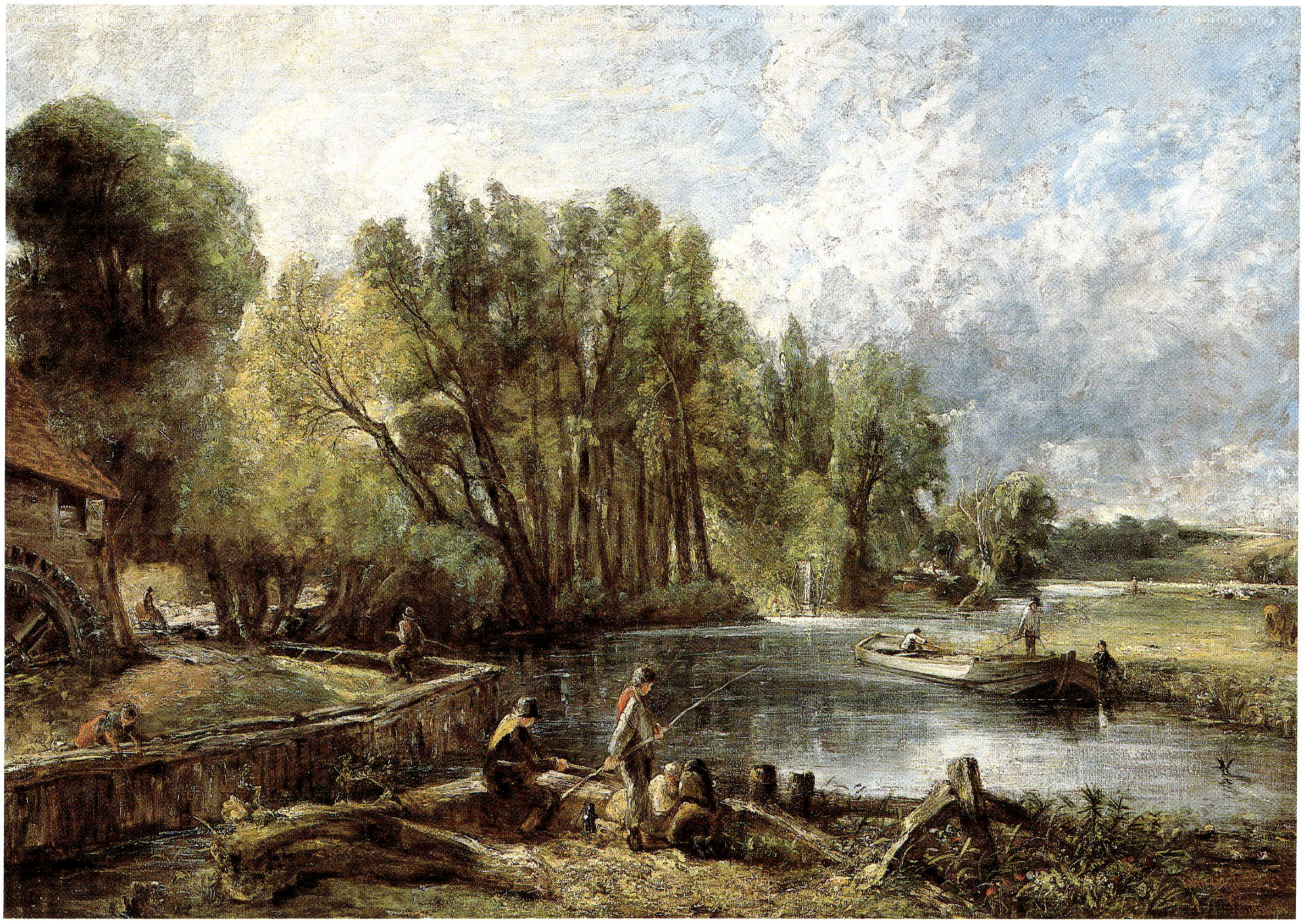

7. John Constable, R.A., *Stratford Mill*, 'The Young Waltonians', CAT. 9

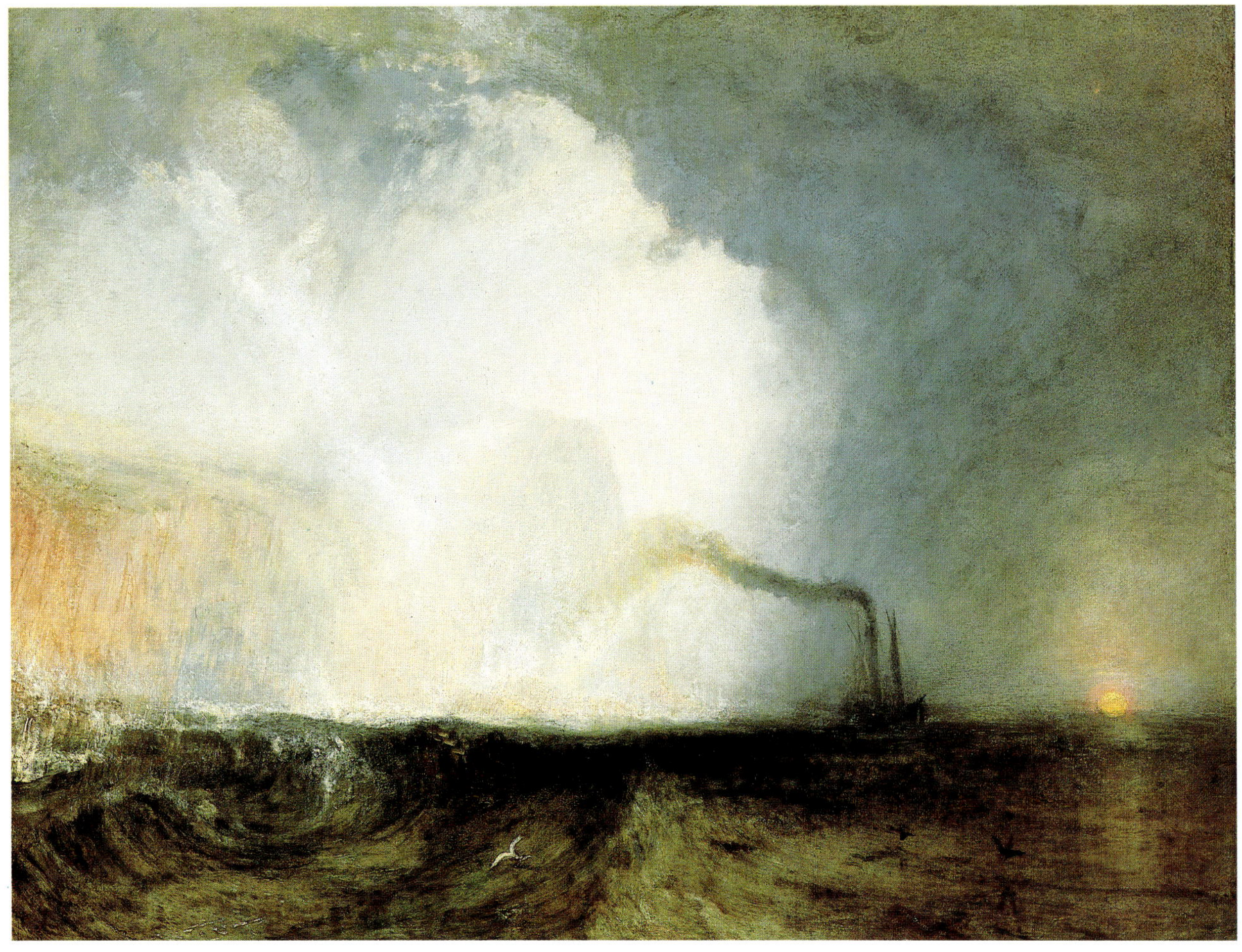

8. J.M.W. Turner, *Staffa, Fingal's Cave*, CAT. 53

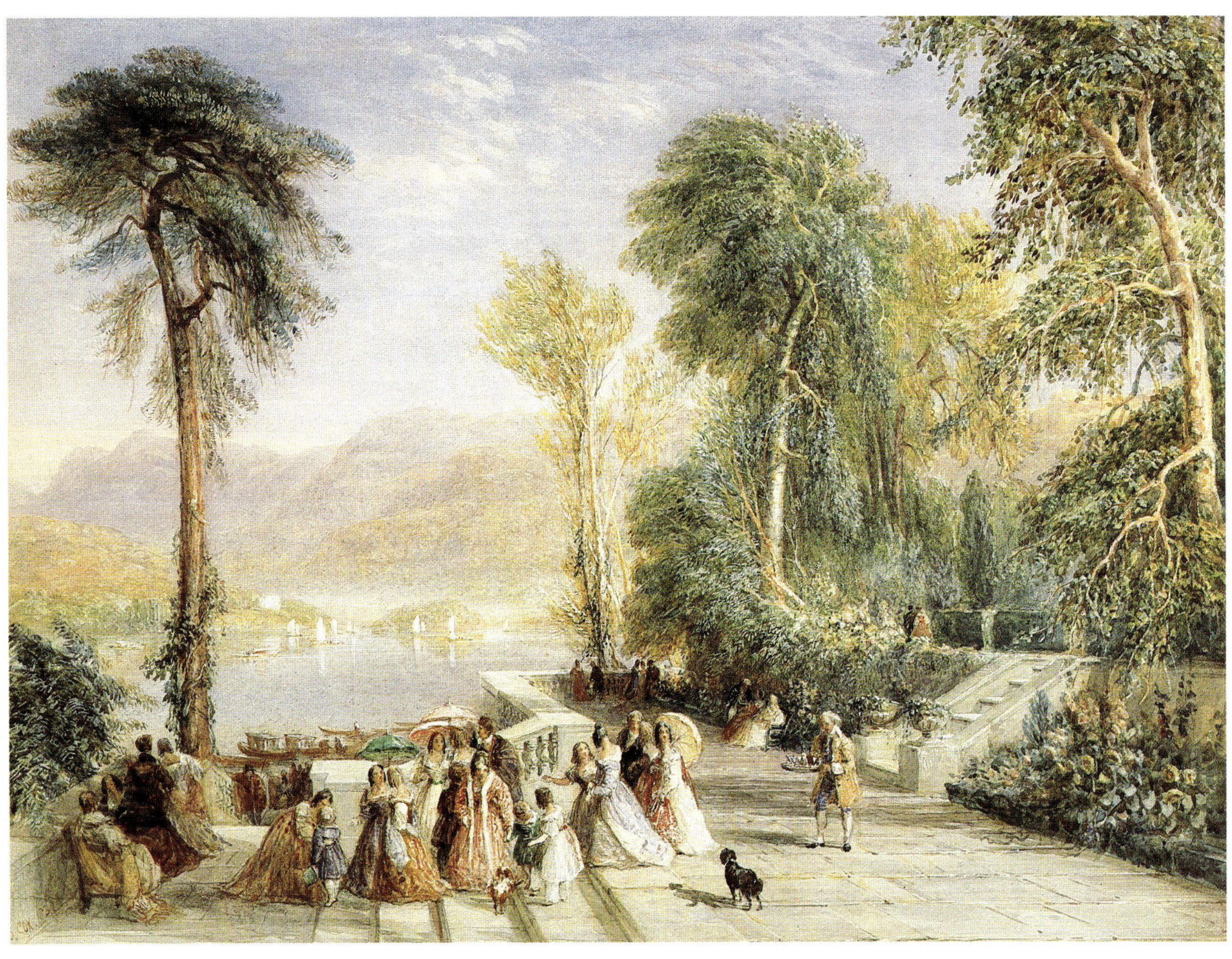

9. David Cox (The Elder), *Windermere during the Regatta*, CAT. 78

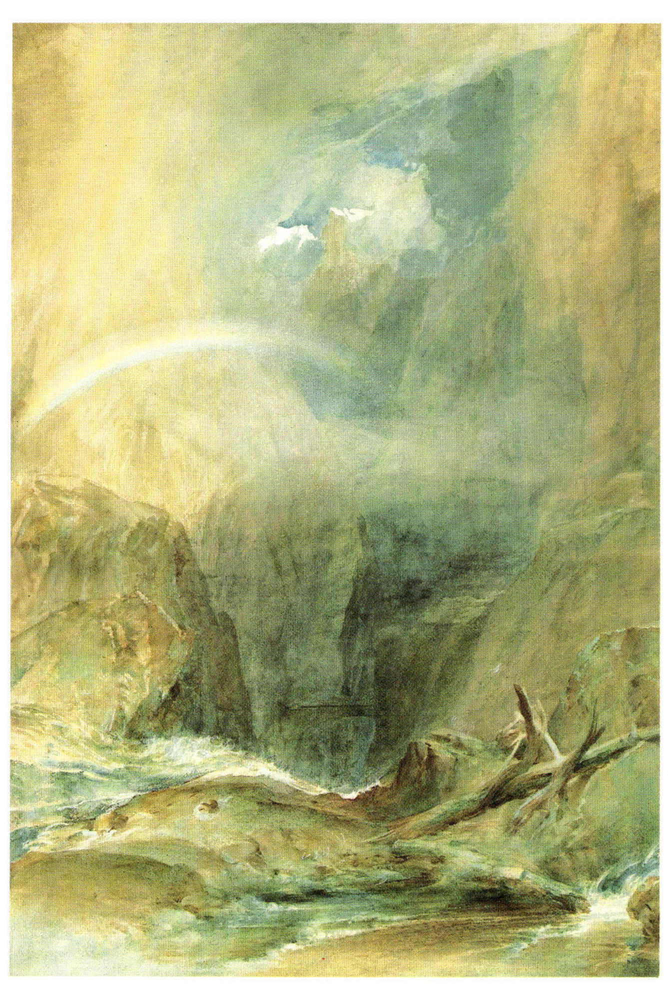

10. J.M.W. Turner, *The Devil's Bridge*, CAT. 127

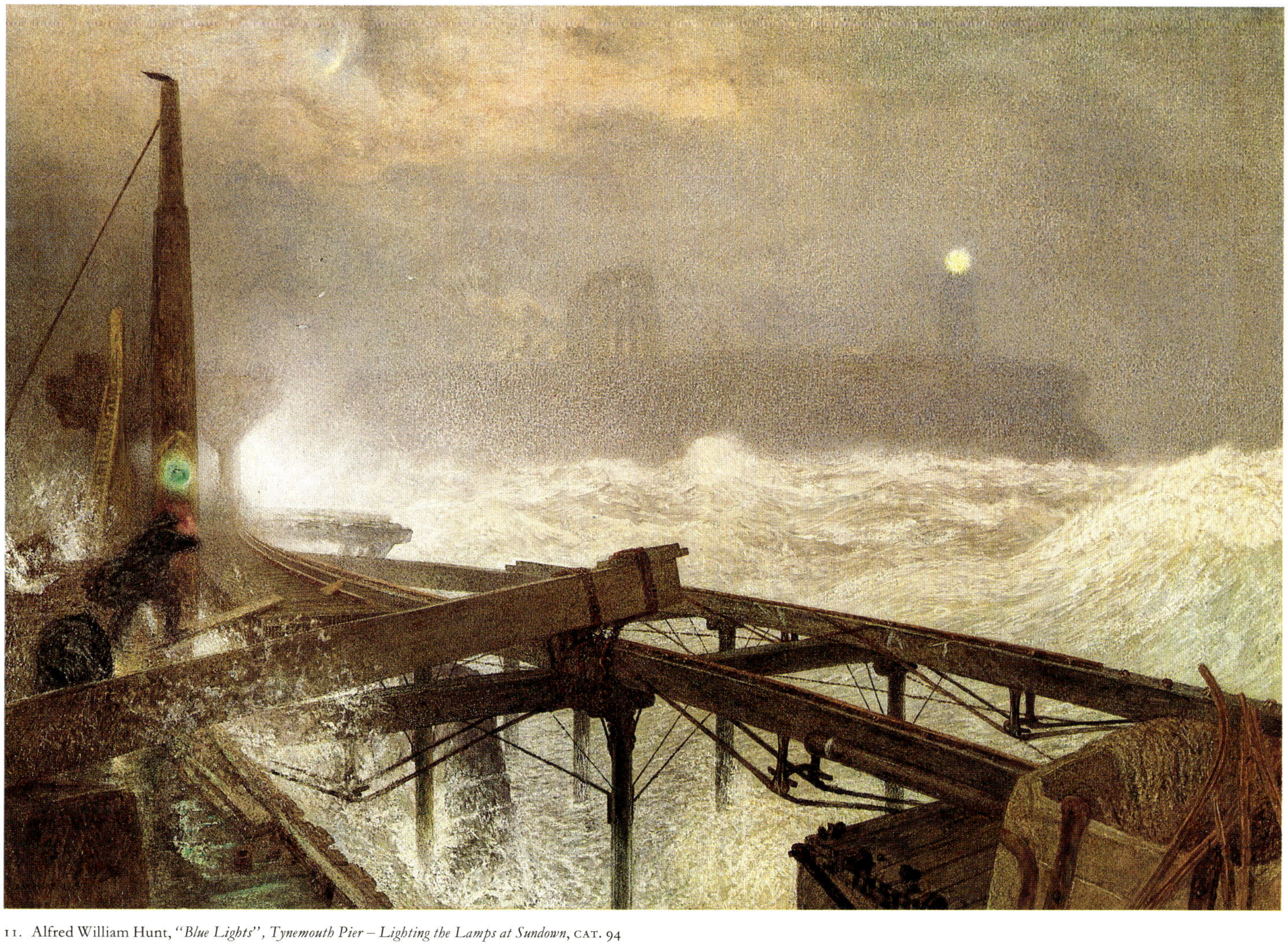

11. Alfred William Hunt, *"Blue Lights", Tynemouth Pier – Lighting the Lamps at Sundown*, CAT. 94

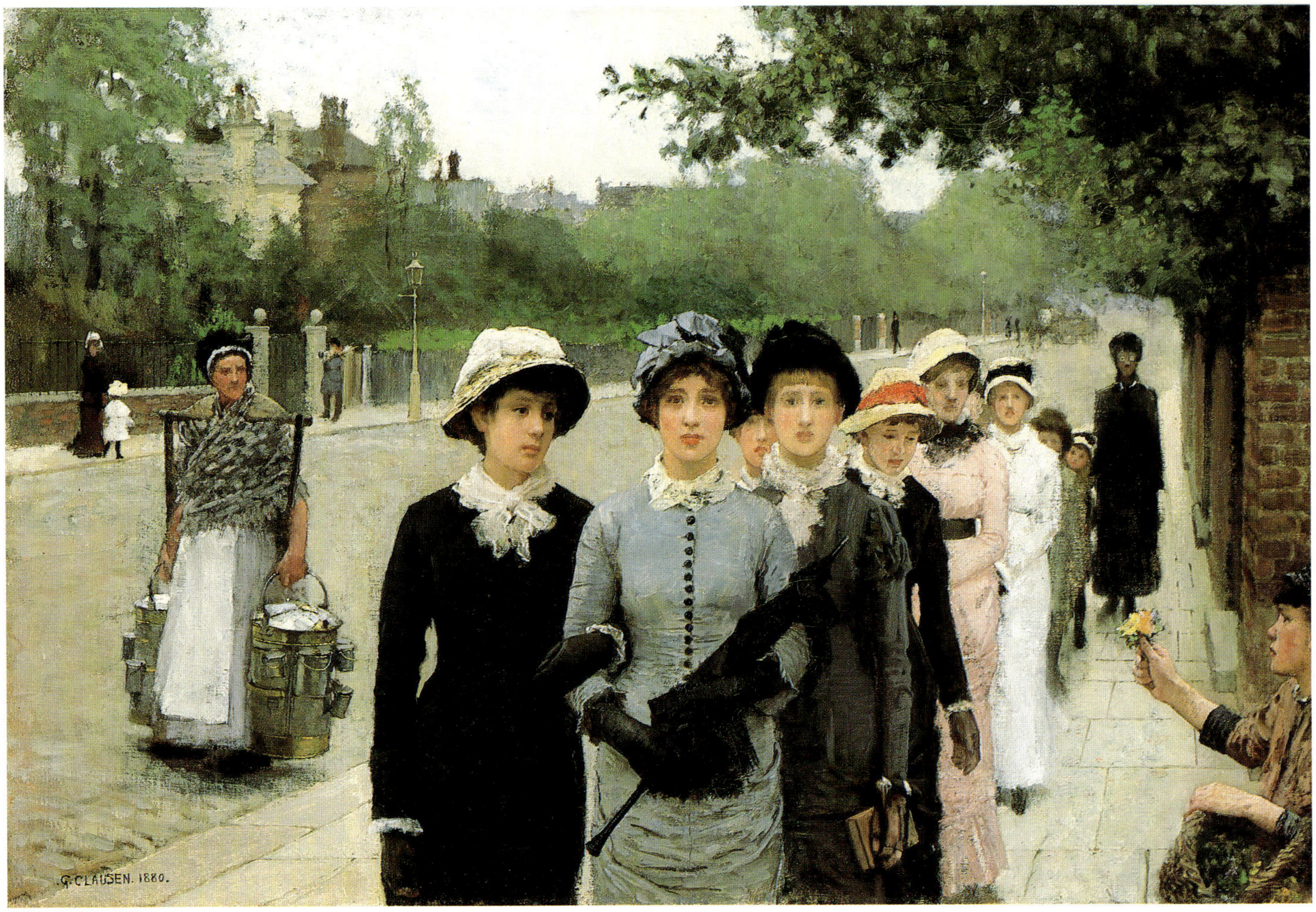

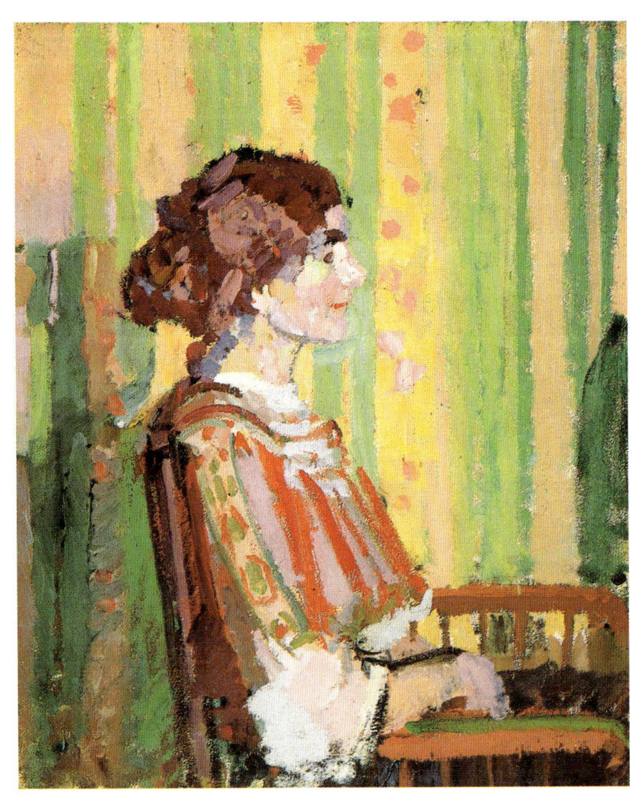

13. Harold Gilman, *Mrs. Robert Bevan*, CAT. 19

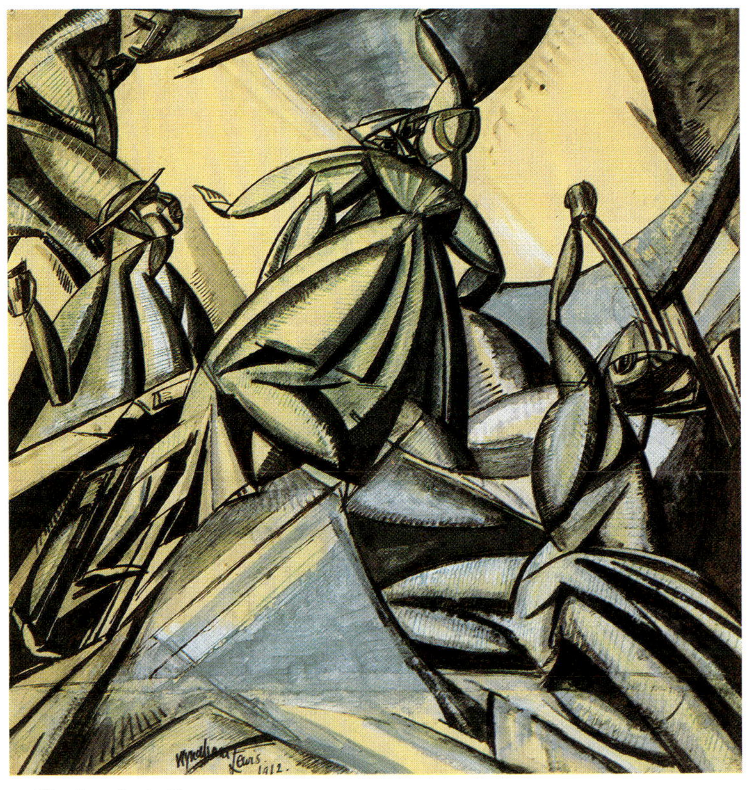

14. Wyndham Lewis, *Kermesse*, CAT. 104

12. Sir George Clausen, R.A., *Schoolgirls*, CAT. 6

PAINTINGS AND SCULPTURE

No collection of art can ever hope to be entirely representative of all that is best in any particular field. The arbitrary way in which works become available, or suddenly unavailable if, say, an export licence is refused, can thwart the most comprehensive of plans. Nevertheless, the collection of British paintings established by Paul Mellon has already acquired the enviable reputation of not only displaying an impeccable personal taste, with intimate moments of rare beauty, but also answering the demands of an encyclopaedic representation of the history of British art.

Since the Center opened in 1977 the painting collection has increased by one hundred and eleven works, in addition to those generously made over to Yale which were already in Paul Mellon's collection. All the acquisitions of paintings up to the summer of 1985 are listed in detail in *A Concise Catalogue of Paintings*, published in that year, but certain general points can be made about the acquisitions of the last ten years.

First, there are a number of absolutely outstanding works which rival the best in the collection. Among these the Gainsborough of *Johnstone-Pulteney*, the Hogarth of *The Jeffreys Family* (Fig.6), the Rubens *Peace Embracing Plenty* (Fig.10), Constable's *Stratford Mill* (Col. Fig.7), and the two Turners, *The Wreckers*, and *Staffa* (Col. Fig.8) will remain permanent reminders of Paul Mellon's generosity. Complementing these, minor masterpieces of great individual charm have been acquired, of which *The Children in an Interior* by Arthur Devis (Fig.5), *The Cowper-Gore Family* by Zoffany, the Ramsay of *An Unknown Woman* (Col. Fig.4), and the Paul Sandby of *Hackwood Park* are typical of this aspect of the Mellon Collection. They represent in an immediate way the civilised qualities of Georgian culture, with no great pretensions to 'historical' posturing.

The collection has, however, expanded into major areas which were perceived to be under-represented. The sixteenth and seventeenth centuries have been added to, with Robert Peake's only signed work, a fine Hans Eworth (Col. Fig.1), one of van Somer's portraits of *James I*, a rare Kierincx view of *Richmond, Yorkshire*, painted for Charles I whose cipher it bears, three paintings from the reign of Charles II by Lely, including the appealing *Countess of Oxford* (Col. Fig.2), and three paintings by his best known disciple, Willem Wissing, which may be enough for any collection of British art. It may be pointed out that the Center has equally been frustrated through export restrictions of other seventeenth-century works – a Dobson, a Lely sketch of James II, and a large Clostermans.

The nineteenth century has also received attention. A full-length Lawrence from the beginning of the century (Fig.7), a Geddes of a Scottish sitter in 'Syriac' costume, and the overpowering Martin of *The Deluge* are varied examples of romantic imagery. The Victorian period was an obvious case for further thought, but the change of taste which had made it more fashionable had also made it more expensive. Nevertheless, significant examples have been acquired: Augustus Egg's moral diptych of *The Life and Death of Buckingham*, J.E. Millais' *L'Enfant du Régiment* (Fig.8), and works by George Richmond (Fig.9), Alma-Tadema, Frederick Sandys, Poynter, and Albert Moore, for example, range over the variety of Victorian styles, including that of Pre-Raphaelitism. From this period it is fitting that the late Jane Ritchie gave in 1981 a Creswick of *The Terrace at Haddon Hall* (Fig.4), 1840, in memory of her husband, Andrew Carnduff Ritchie, the Director of the Yale University Art Gallery, 1957-1971, who had done so much for British art, and who had been instrumental in suggesting that Yale would be a suitable repository for the Paul Mellon Collection.

With paintings by Clausen (Col. Fig.12), Fred Hall, and Frank Holl, the new realism at the end of the nineteenth century is also represented. The acquisition of significant examples of late nineteenth-century and twentieth-century works by the leading 'modern' artists of the period is a new departure for the Center. A fine group of Sickerts (Fig.11) introduce his followers in the Camden Town Group, Spencer Gore, Charles Ginner, and Harold Gilman, by whom a particularly fine portrait of *Mrs Bevan* (Col. Fig.13) has recently been given by Paul Mellon. These are displayed alongside their contemporaries of the Bloomsbury group, Vanessa Bell (Fig.2), Duncan Grant, and its principal theorist, Roger Fry, while other leading British artists of the twentieth century, such as Matthew Smith, Paul Nash, and Stanley Spencer, have followed logically. Most recently, Paul Mellon has made an outstanding gift of four paintings by Ben Nicholson (cover illustration).

These modern acquisitions, not perhaps originally envisaged when the collection was begun, do not mean that the golden age of British painting has been ignored. Charming minor portraits, by the interesting Irishman, Thomas Frye, of *Mrs Wardle* , 1742; a full length of *John Dodd, M.P.*, 1739, by John Vanderbank; a very early work by Reynolds of *An Unknown Naval Officer*, c. 1748, and a fascinating unfinished Mengs of *George 3rd Earl Cowper* are interesting works for study. Sculpture, too, has not been neglected, with pieces by Gott, Lord Leighton, Gibson, Wilton, Nollekens, Scheemakers, Barbara Hepworth and Henry Moore (Fig.13). The following selection is an attempt to show some of the most outstanding of all these acquisitions, as well as revealing the byways that such a collection can explore.

MALCOLM CORMACK
Curator of Paintings

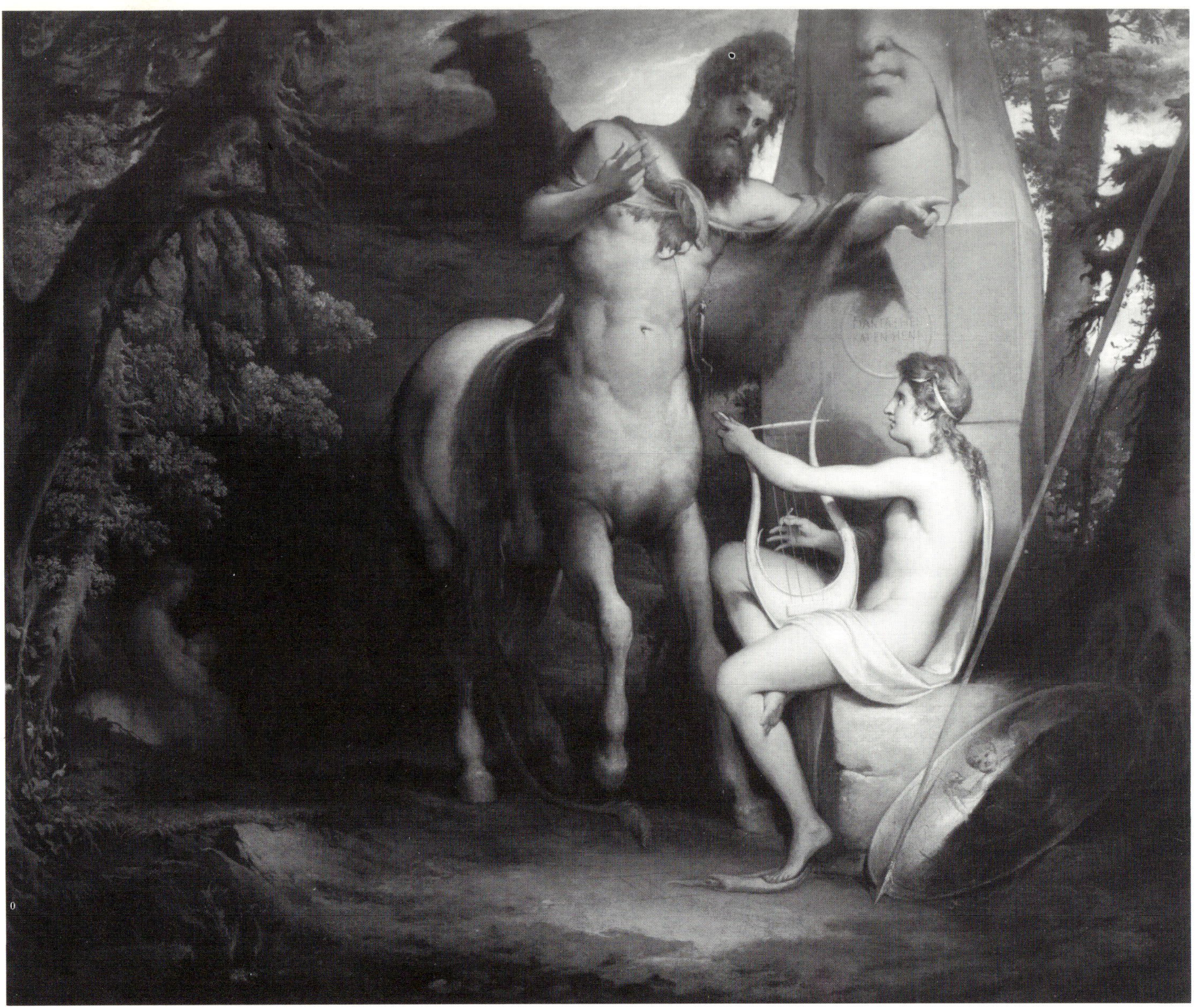

1. James Barry, R.A., *The Education of Achilles*, CAT. 1

1. JAMES BARRY, R.A. (1741-1806)

The Education of Achilles, c. 1772

Oil on canvas
$40\frac{1}{2} \times 50\frac{3}{4}$ in. (103.0 × 129.0 cm.)

Acquired Paul Mellon Fund 1978
B1978.6 **(Fig.1)**

2. VANESSA BELL (1879-1961)

Self-Portrait, c. 1915

Oil on canvas laid on panel
$25\frac{1}{8} \times 18\frac{1}{16}$ in. (63.7 × 46.2 cm.)

Acquired Paul Mellon Fund 1982
B1982.16.2 **(Fig.2)**

3. SIR FRANK WILLIAM BRANGWYN, R.A. (1867-1956)

Departure of the Bucintoro

Oil on canvas
52×69 in. (132.0 × 175.2 cm.)

Gift of Joseph F. McCrindle 1982
B1982.33

4. STEPHEN BUCKLEY (b. 1944)

Concluding 8, 1977

Liquitex on canvas
80×69 in. (193.2 × 175.2 cm.)

Gift of Barbara Gladstone 1985
B1985.34

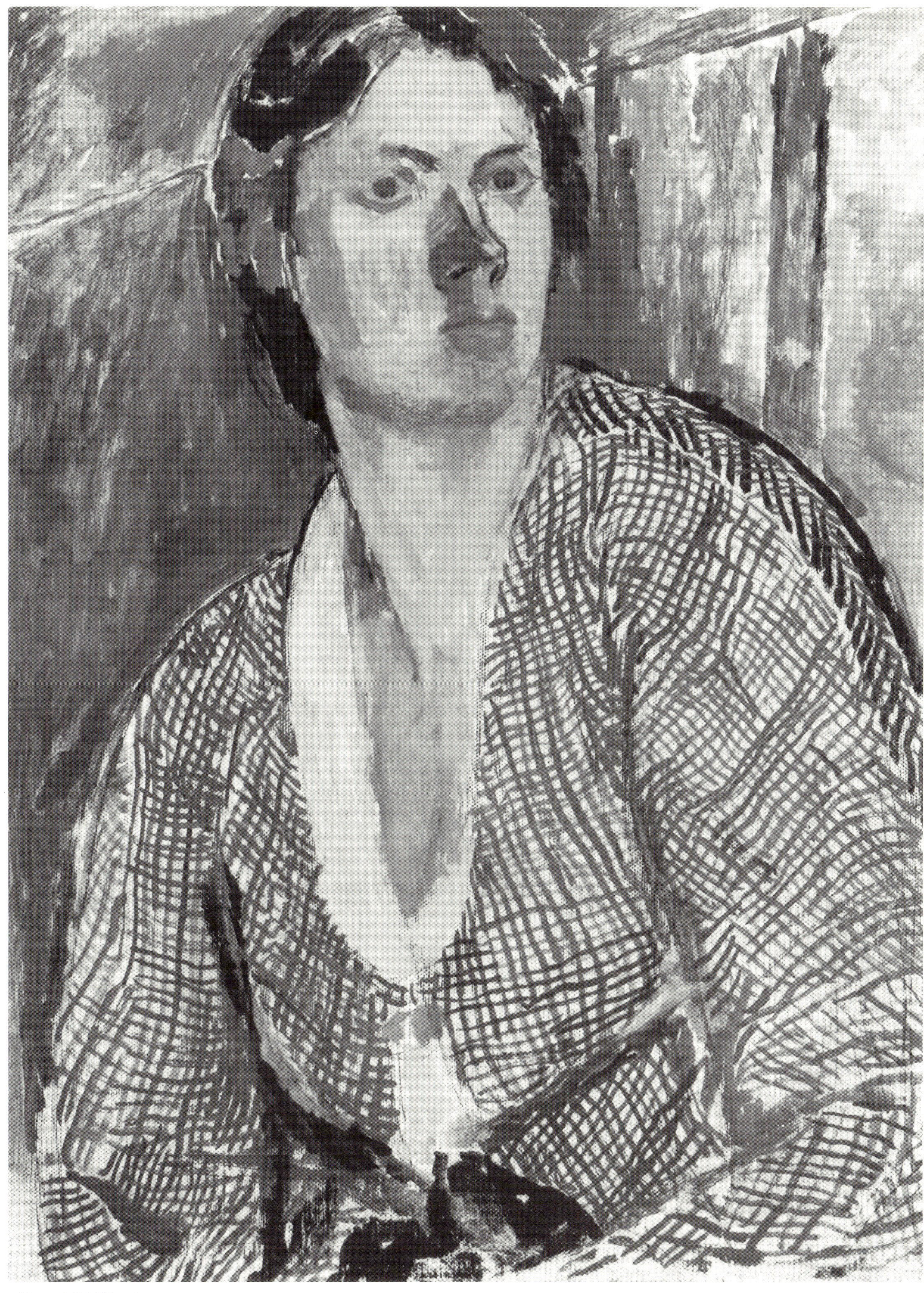

2. Vanessa Bell, *Self-Portrait*, CAT. 2

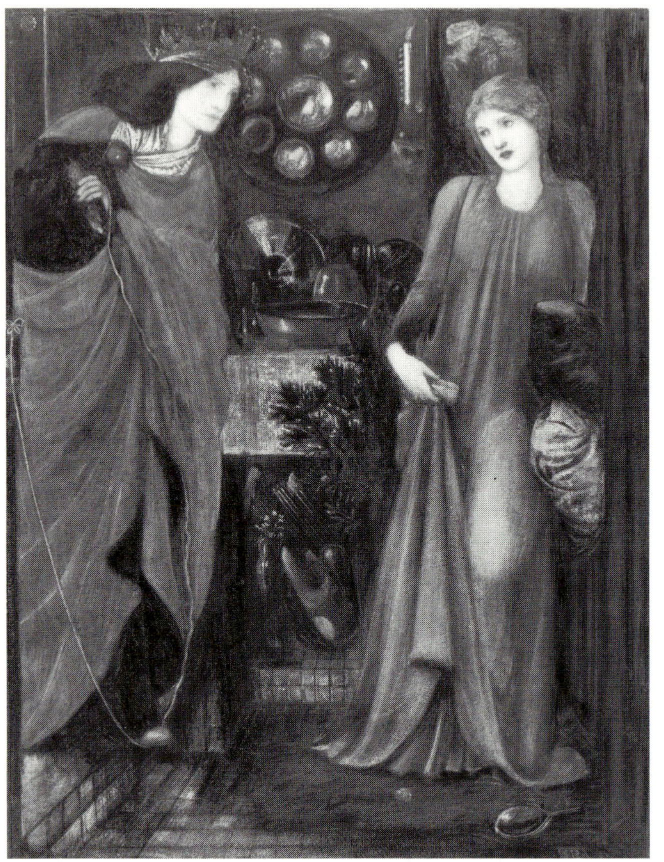

3. Sir Edward Coley Burne-Jones, *Fair Rosamund and Queen Eleanor*, CAT. 5

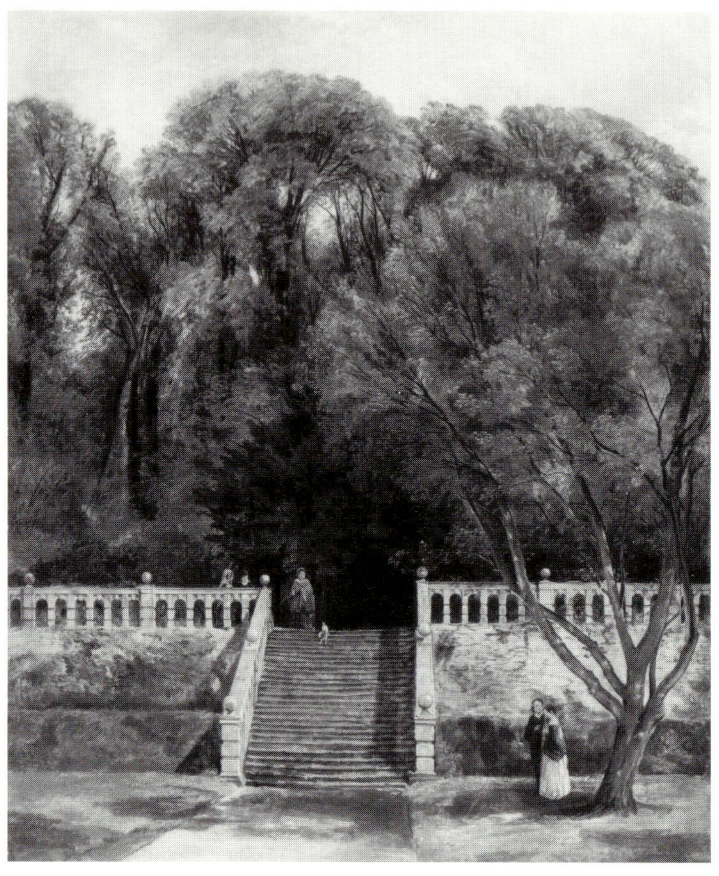

4. Thomas Creswick, R.A., *On the Terrace at Haddon Hall, Derbyshire*, CAT. 11

5. SIR EDWARD COLEY BURNE-JONES (1833-1898)

Fair Rosamund and Queen Eleanor, signed and dated 1861

Mixed media with gold on paper
$19\frac{1}{2} \times 14\frac{3}{4}$ in. (49.5 × 37.5 cm.)
Acquired Paul Mellon Fund 1980
B1980.24 **(Fig.3)**

6. SIR GEORGE CLAUSEN, R.A. (1852-1944)

Schoolgirls, signed and dated 1880

Oil on canvas
$20\frac{1}{2} \times 30\frac{3}{8}$ in. (52.1 × 77.2 cm.)
Gift of Paul Mellon 1985
B1985.10.1 **(Colour Fig.12. Page 8)**

7. SAMUEL COLMAN (fl. 1816-1840)

The Mysterious Island, 1837

Oil on canvas
$24\frac{1}{8} \times 29\frac{1}{4}$ in. (61.3 × 74.3 cm.)
Acquired Paul Mellon Fund 1986
B1986.11.1

8. JOHN CONSTABLE, R.A. (1776-1837)

Malvern Hall, Warwickshire, c. 1820-21

Oil on canvas
$21\frac{1}{2} \times 30\frac{3}{4}$ in. (54.0 × 78.0 cm.)
Paul Mellon Collection 1977
B1977.14.43

9. JOHN CONSTABLE, R.A. (1776-1837)

Stratford Mill, 'The Young Waltonians', c. 1820

Oil on canvas
$51\frac{1}{2} \times 72\frac{1}{2}$ in. (131.0 × 184.0 cm.)
Acquired Paul Mellon Fund 1983
B1983.18 **(Colour Fig.7. Page 5)**

10. JOHN SINGLETON COPLEY, R.A. (1738-1815)

Richard Heber, 1782

Oil on canvas
$65\frac{1}{4} \times 51\frac{3}{16}$ in. (165.7 × 130.0 cm.)
Paul Mellon Collection 1979
B1981.25.745

11. THOMAS CRESWICK, R.A. (1811-1869)

On the Terrace at Haddon Hall, Derbyshire,
signed and dated 1840

Oil on panel
24 × 20 in. (60.9 × 50.8 cm.)
Gift of Jane Ritchie in memory of Andrew Carnduff Ritchie 1981
B1981.14 **(Fig.4)**

12. ARTHUR DEVIS (c. 1711-1787)

Children in an Interior, c. 1742-43

Oil on canvas
$39 \times 49\frac{3}{4}$ in. (99.0 × 125.5 cm.)
Paul Mellon Collection 1978
B1978.43.5 **(Fig.5)**

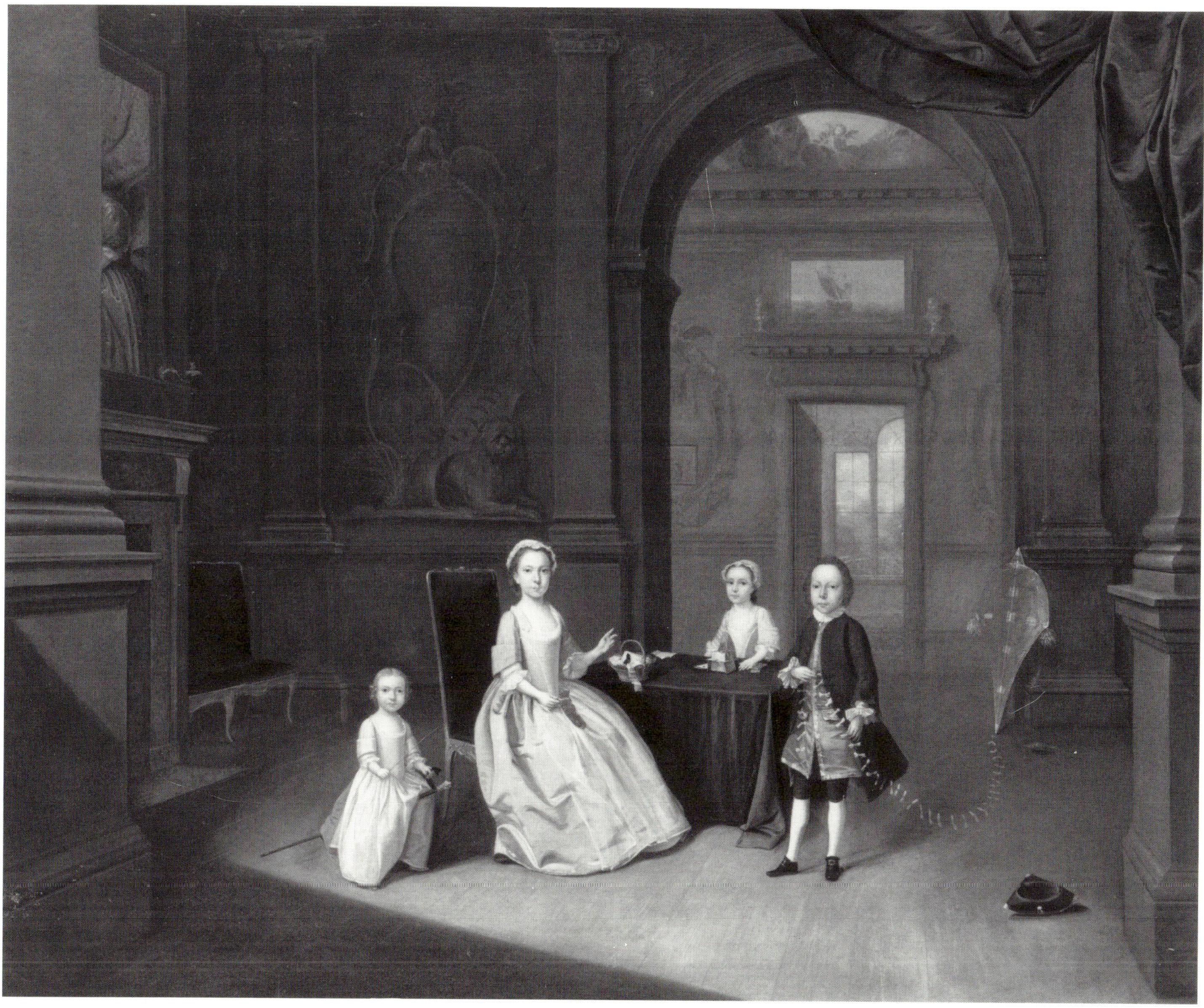

5. Arthur Devis, *Children in an Interior*, CAT. 12

13. AUGUSTUS LEOPOLD EGG, R.A. (1816-1863)

The Life of Buckingham, 1854

Oil on canvas
$29\frac{1}{2} \times 36$ in. (74.9 × 91.4 cm.)
Paul Mellon Collection 1978
B1978.43.7

14. AUGUSTUS LEOPOLD EGG, R.A. (1816-1863)

The Death of Buckingham, 1854

Oil on canvas
$29\frac{1}{2} \times 36$ in. (74.9 × 91.4 cm.)
Paul Mellon Collection 1978
B1978.43.6

15. HANS EWORTH (fl. 1540-1573)

Portrait of a Woman, possibly Mary Fitzalan, Duchess of Norfolk, c. 1555(?)

Oil on panel
$37 \times 28\frac{3}{4}$ in. (94.0 × 73.0 cm.)
Acquired Paul Mellon Fund 1986
B1986.9   **(Colour Fig.1. Page 2)**

16. THOMAS GAINSBOROUGH, R.A. (1727-1788)

Mr. and Mrs. John Gravenor and their Daughters, Elizabeth and Dorothea, c. 1747

Oil on canvas
$35\frac{1}{2} \times 35\frac{1}{2}$ in. (90.1 × 90.1 cm.)
Paul Mellon Collection 1977
B1977.14.56   **(Colour Fig.5. Page 4)**

17. THOMAS GAINSBOROUGH, R.A. (1727-1788)

William Johnstone-Pulteney, later 5th Baronet, c. 1772

Oil on canvas
$93\frac{1}{2} \times 59$ in. (237.5 × 149.8 cm.)
Paul Mellon Collection 1980
B1981.25.734

18. HAROLD GILMAN (1876-1919)

Sylvia Darning, signed, 1917

Oil on canvas
$16\frac{1}{4} \times 18\frac{1}{4}$ in. (41.3 × 46.4 cm.)
Paul Mellon Collection 1981
B1981.25.735

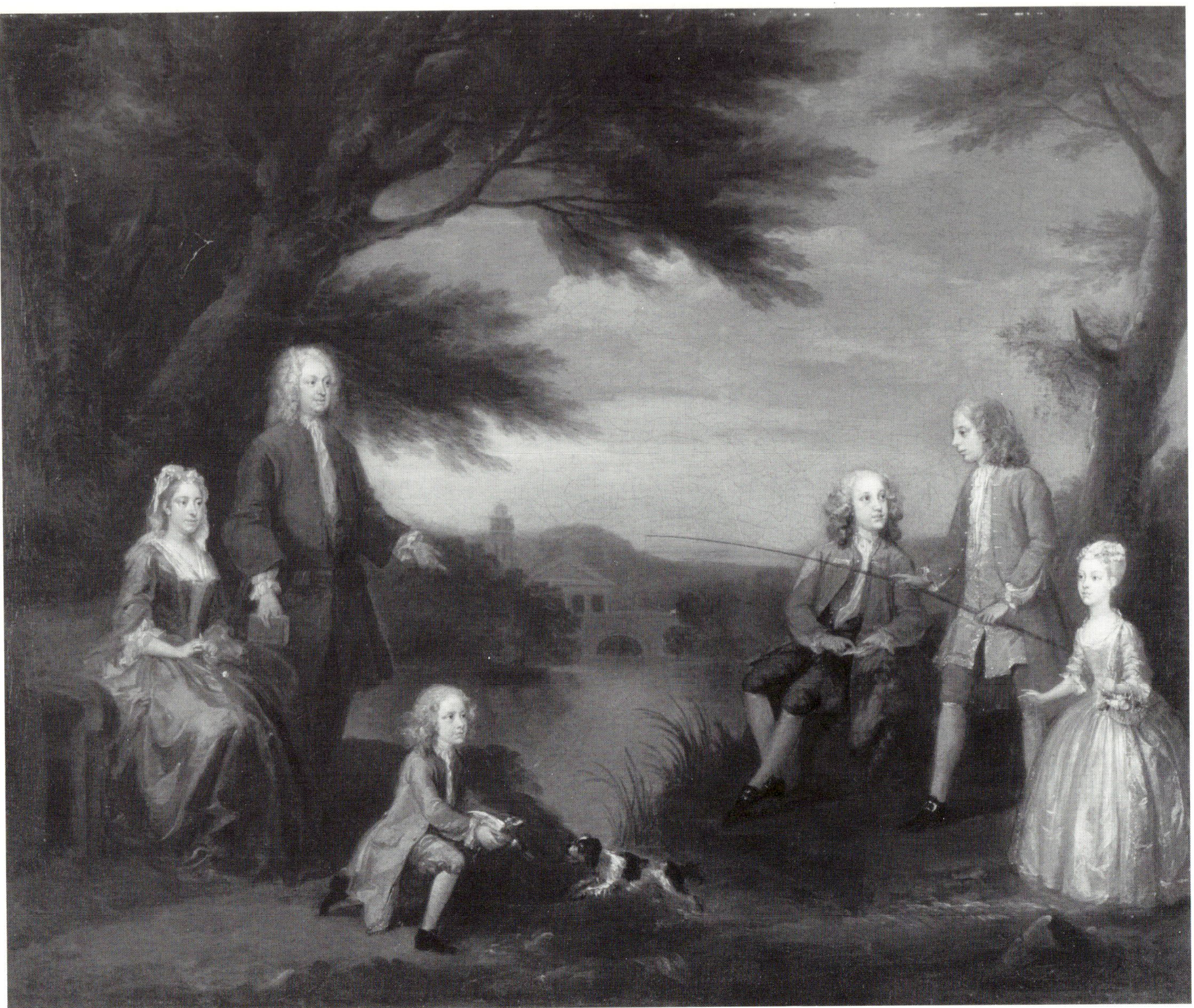

6. William Hogarth, *The Jeffreys Family*, CAT. 26

19. HAROLD GILMAN (1876-1919)

Mrs. Robert Bevan, c. 1913

Oil on canvas
24 × 20 in. (60.9 × 50.8 cm.)
Acquired Paul Mellon Fund 1985
B1986.1.1   **(Colour Fig.13. Page 8)**

20. CHARLES GINNER (1878-1952)

Design for Tiger-Hunting Mural in the Cabaret Theatre Club, 1912

Oil and pencil on card
$13\frac{1}{2} \times 22\frac{5}{8}$ in. (34.0 × 57.5 cm.)
Acquired Paul Mellon Fund 1985
B1985.3.2

21. SPENCER FREDERICK GORE (1878-1914)

Tennis at Hertingfordbury, signed, 1910

Oil on canvas
$15\frac{15}{16} \times 20$ in. (40.5 × 50.8 cm.)
Acquired Paul Mellon Fund 1980
B1980.32

22. SPENCER FREDERICK GORE (1878-1914)

Cambrian Road, Richmond, signed, 1913-14

Oil on canvas
16 × 20 in. (40.6 × 50.8 cm.)
Acquired Paul Mellon Fund 1983
B1983.11.1

23. SPENCER FREDERICK GORE (1878-1914)

Design for Deer-Hunting Mural in the Cabaret Theatre Club, 1912

Oil and chalk on paper
11 × 24 in. (28.0 × 61.0 cm.)
Acquired Paul Mellon Fund 1985
B1985.3.1

24. DUNCAN GRANT (1885-1978)

In Memoriam: Rupert Brooke, 1915

Oil and collage on panel
$21\frac{9}{16} \times 11\frac{3}{4}$ in. (54.7 × 29.8 cm.)
Acquired Paul Mellon Fund 1985
B1985.3.3

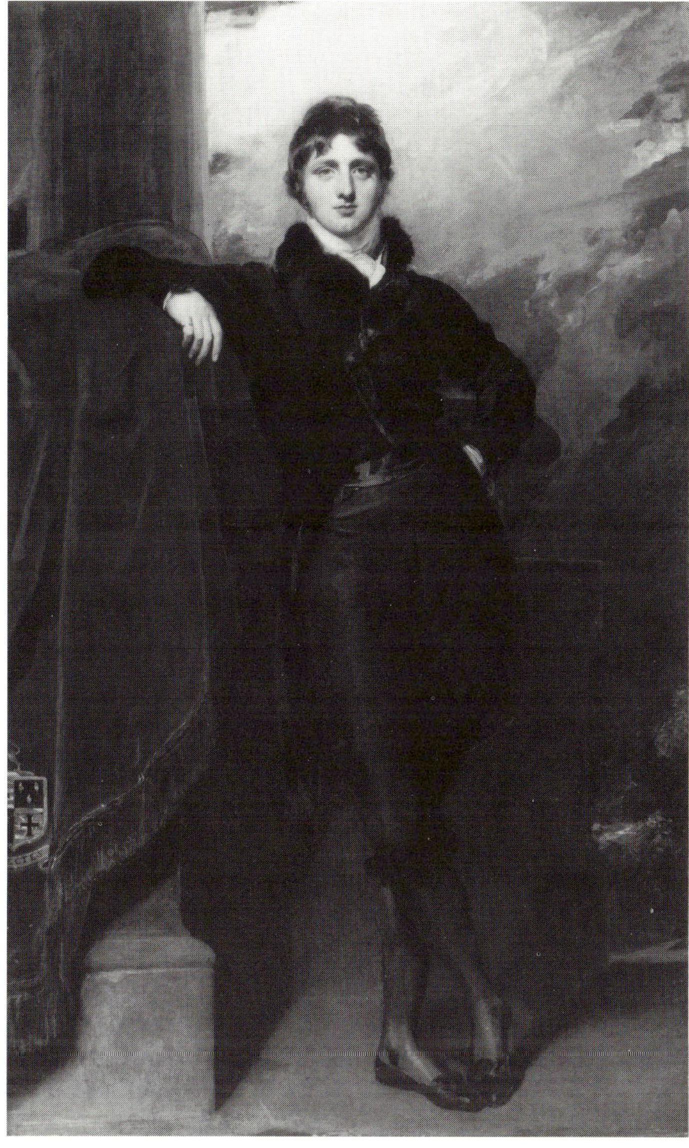

7. Sir Thomas Lawrence, P.R.A., *Lord Granville Leveson-Gower, later 1st Earl Granville*, CAT. 32

25. WILLIAM HOGARTH (1697-1764)

William Augustus, Duke of Cumberland, dated 1732

Oil on canvas
$18\frac{7}{8} \times 13\frac{7}{8}$ in. (35.2 × 47.7 cm.)
Paul Mellon Collection 1977
B1977.14.59

26. WILLIAM HOGARTH (1697-1764)

The Jeffreys Family, 1730

Oil on canvas
$28\frac{1}{4} \times 35\frac{3}{4}$ in. (72.0 × 91.0 cm.)
Acquired Paul Mellon Fund 1981
B1981.20 **(Fig.6)**

27. JOHN HOPPNER, R.A. (1758-1810)

An Unknown British Officer, probably of 11th (North Devonshire) Regiment of Foot, c. 1800

Oil on canvas
30 × 25 in. (76.2 × 63.5 cm.)
Gift of Mrs. Charles F. Samson in memory of Charles F. Samson, Yale College, Class of 1902, 1977
B1977.3

28. JOHN WILLIAM INCHBOLD (1830-1888)

A View at Ariccia, signed and dated 1860

Oil on panel
8 × 12 in. (20.3 × 30.8 cm.)
Acquired Paul Mellon Fund 1982
B1982.2

29. JAMES DICKSON INNES (1887-1914)

Landscape with a Grazing Horse, signed, c. 1912-13

Oil on panel
$12\frac{11}{16} \times 16$ in. (32.4 × 40.6 cm.)
Acquired Joseph H. Ryder Fund 1985
B1985.8

30. ANGELICA MARIA CATHERINE KAUFFMAN, R.A. (1741-1807)

A Woman, called Lady Hervey, c.1780(?)

Oil on canvas
$29\frac{5}{16} \times 22\frac{7}{8}$ in. (74.5 × 58.1 cm.)
Paul Mellon Collection 1979
B1981.25.755

31. ALEXANDER KEIRINCX (1600-1652)
(also called CARINGS, CIERINX etc.)

Richmond Castle, Yorkshire, signed, c. 1640-41

Oil on panel
18 × 27 in. (45.7 × 68.5 cm.)
Acquired Paul Mellon Fund 1978
B1978.4

32. SIR THOMAS LAWRENCE, P.R.A. (1769-1830)

Lord Granville Leveson-Gower, later 1st Earl Granville, c. 1804-06

Oil on canvas
$92\frac{1}{2} \times 51\frac{1}{2}$ in. (235.0 × 146.0 cm.)
Paul Mellon Collection 1981
B1981.25.736 **(Fig.7)**

33. EDWARD LEAR (1812-1888)

Corfu from Ascension, signed, c. 1856-64

Oil on canvas
$13\frac{1}{2} \times 21\frac{1}{2}$ in. (34.3 × 54.6 cm.)
Gift of Mr. and Mrs. Michael Coe 1979
B1979.11

34. FREDERIC, LORD LEIGHTON, P.R.A. (1830-1896)

Mrs. James Guthrie, c. 1864-65

Oil on canvas
$82\frac{15}{16} \times 54\frac{1}{2}$ in. (210.7 × 138.5 cm.)
Paul Mellon Collection 1978
B1978.43.10

35. SIR PETER LELY (1618-1680)

Diana Kirke, later Countess of Oxford, c. 1665-70

Oil on canvas
52 × 41 in. (135.3 × 108.6 cm.)
Paul Mellon Collection 1979
B1981.25.756 **(Colour Fig.2. Page 4)**

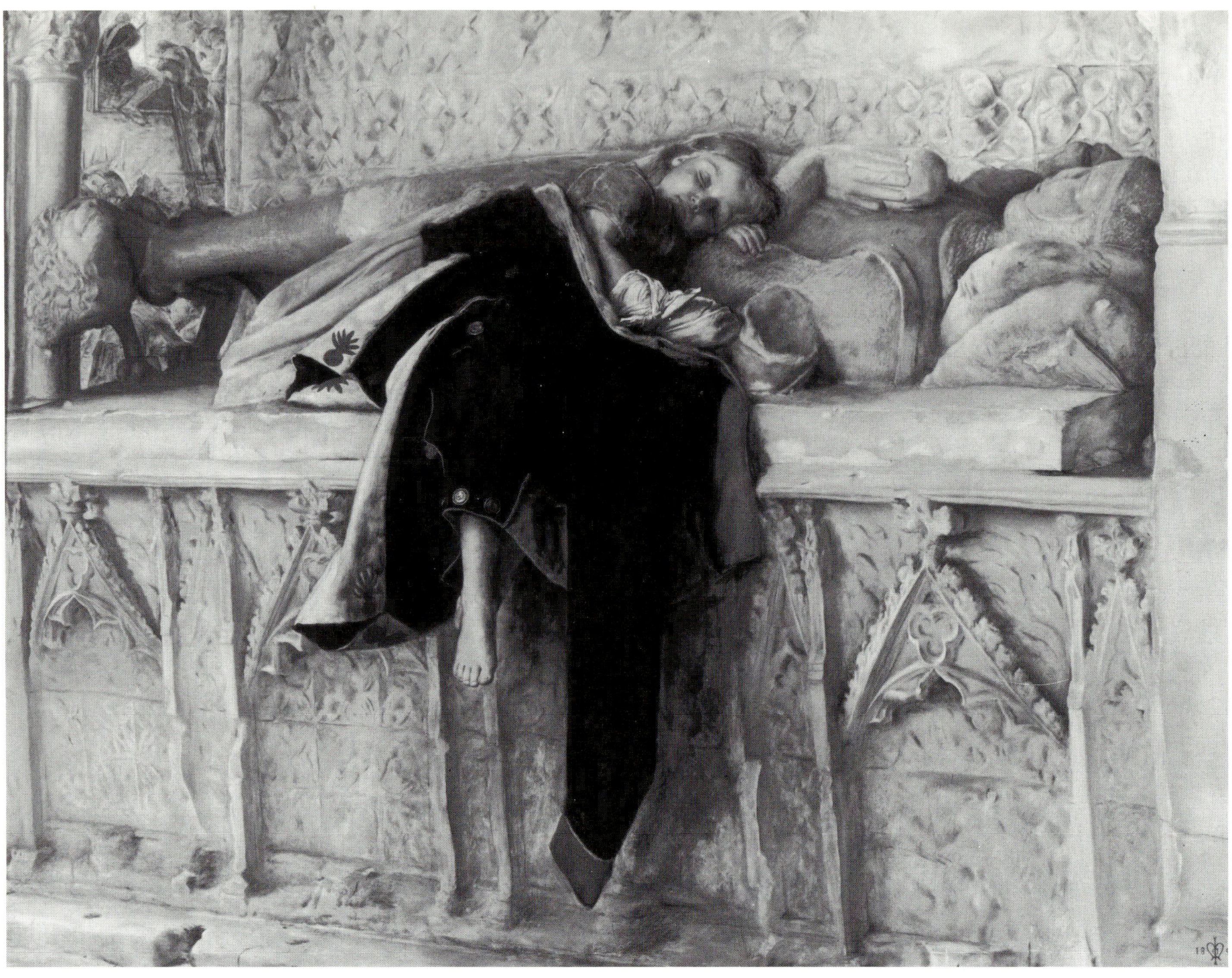

8. Sir John Everett Millais, P.R.A., *L'Enfant du Régiment (The Random Shot)*, CAT. 39

36. SIR PETER LELY (1618-1680)

Edward Montagu, 1st Earl of Sandwich, c.1670

Oil on canvas
$87\frac{7}{8} \times 51\frac{1}{2}$ in. (223.2 × 130.8 cm.)
Acquired Paul Mellon Fund 1980
B1980.25.1

37. CHARLES ROBERT LESLIE, R.A. (1794-1859)

*Slender with the Assistance of Shallow, Courting Anne Page,
'Merry Wives of Windsor', III, iv*, 1825

Oil on canvas
$26\frac{5}{8} \times 31\frac{1}{2}$ in. (67.7 × 77.5 cm.)
Acquired Paul Mellon Fund 1981
B1981.13.2

38. JOHN MARTIN (1789-1854)

The Deluge, apparently signed and dated 1834

Oil on canvas
$66\frac{1}{4} \times 101\frac{3}{4}$ in. (168.5 × 258.6 cm.)
Paul Mellon Collection 1978
B1978.43.11

39. SIR JOHN EVERETT MILLAIS, P.R.A. (1829-1896)

L'Enfant du Régiment (The Random Shot),
signed and dated 1855

Oil on paper laid on board
$17\frac{3}{4} \times 24$ in. (45.3 × 61.0 cm.)
Acquired Paul Mellon Fund 1980
B1981.4 **(Fig.8)**

40. ALBERT JOSEPH MOORE (1841-1893)

A Musician, signed, c. 1867

Oil on canvas
$11\frac{1}{4} \times 15\frac{1}{4}$ in. (28.6 × 38.7 cm.)
Acquired Paul Mellon Fund 1980
B1980.7

41. BEN NICHOLSON (1894-1982)

Still-Life 1929, c. 1929-35

Oil and pencil on canvas
$26\frac{1}{2} \times 32\frac{1}{2}$ in. (67.3 × 82.5 cm.)
Paul Mellon Collection 1982
B1985.19.4

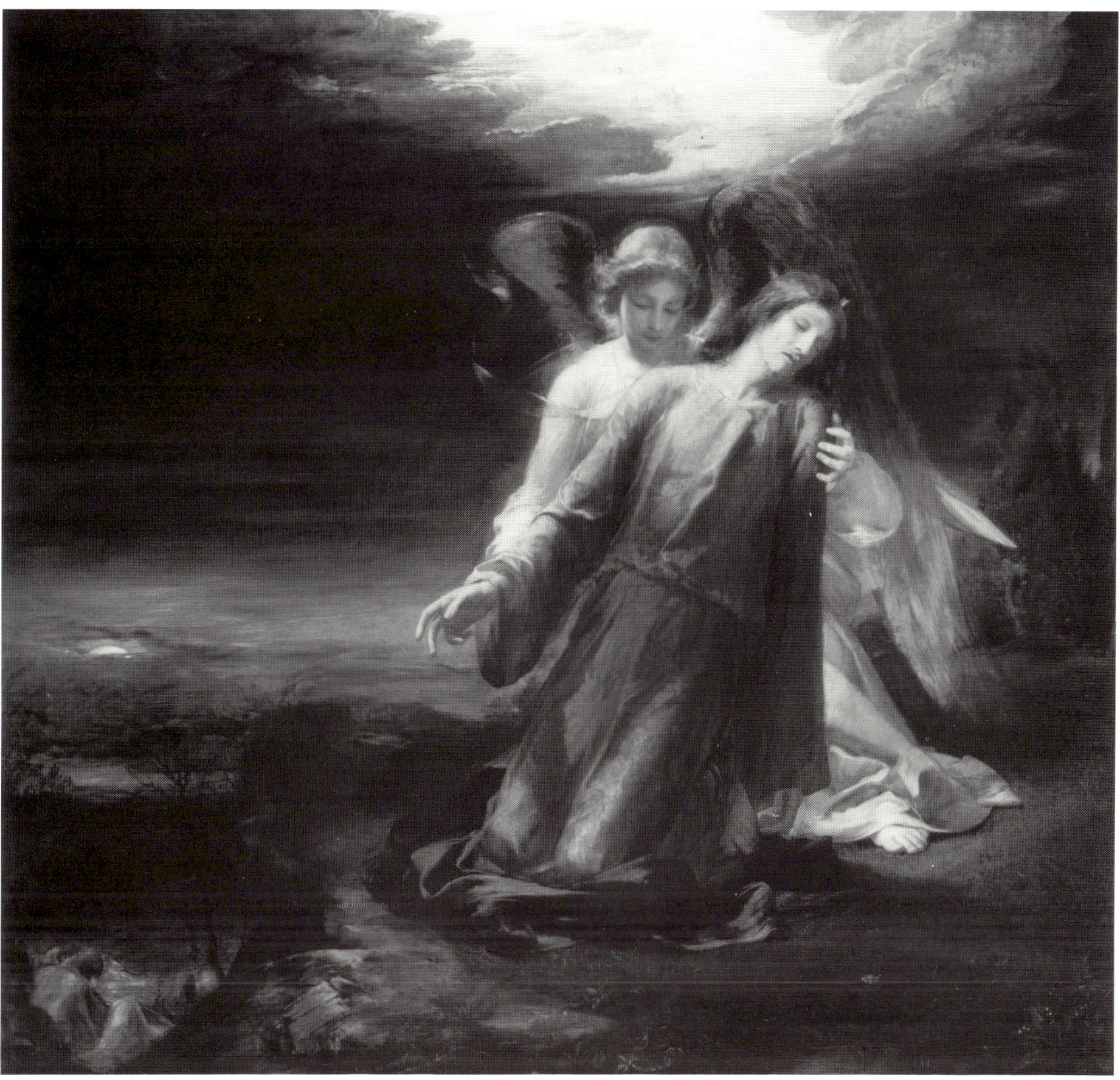

9. George Richmond, R.A., *And there appeared an Angel unto Him from Heaven strengthening Him*, CAT. 46

42. BEN NICHOLSON (1894-1982)

May 1955 (Gwithian)

Oil on canvas
41¾ × 41¾ in. (106.0 × 106.0 cm.)
Paul Mellon Collection 1965
B1985.19.2 **(Cover illustration)**

43. ROBERT PEAKE THE ELDER (c. 1551-1619)

An Unknown Military Commander, Aged 60,
signed and dated 1593

Oil on panel
44½ × 35¼ in. (113.1 × 89.2 cm.)
Acquired Paul Mellon Fund 1979
B1979.16

44. ALLAN RAMSAY (1713-1784)

An Unknown Woman in a Pink Dress, c. 1762

Oil on canvas
30 × 25 3/16 in. (76.2 × 64.0 cm.)
Paul Mellon Collection 1979
B1981.25.761 **(Colour Fig.4. Page 4)**

45. SIR JOSHUA REYNOLDS, P.R.A. (1723-1792)

An Unknown Man, c. 1748

Oil on canvas
30 × 25 in. (76.2 × 63.5 cm.)
Acquired Paul Mellon Fund 1986
B1986.18

46. GEORGE RICHMOND, R.A. (1809-1896)

'And there appeared an Angel unto Him from Heaven,
strengthening Him,' (Luke 22:43), signed, 1858

Oil on panel
41¾ × 46 in. (106.1 × 116.8 cm.)
Acquired Paul Mellon Fund 1983
B1984.8 **(Fig.9)**

47. GEORGE ROMNEY (1734-1802)

Portrait of Mrs. George Wilson and her Daughter, c. 1776-77

Oil on canvas
49 × 39½ in. (124.3 × 100.3 cm.)
Acquired Paul Mellon Fund 1982
B1983.1

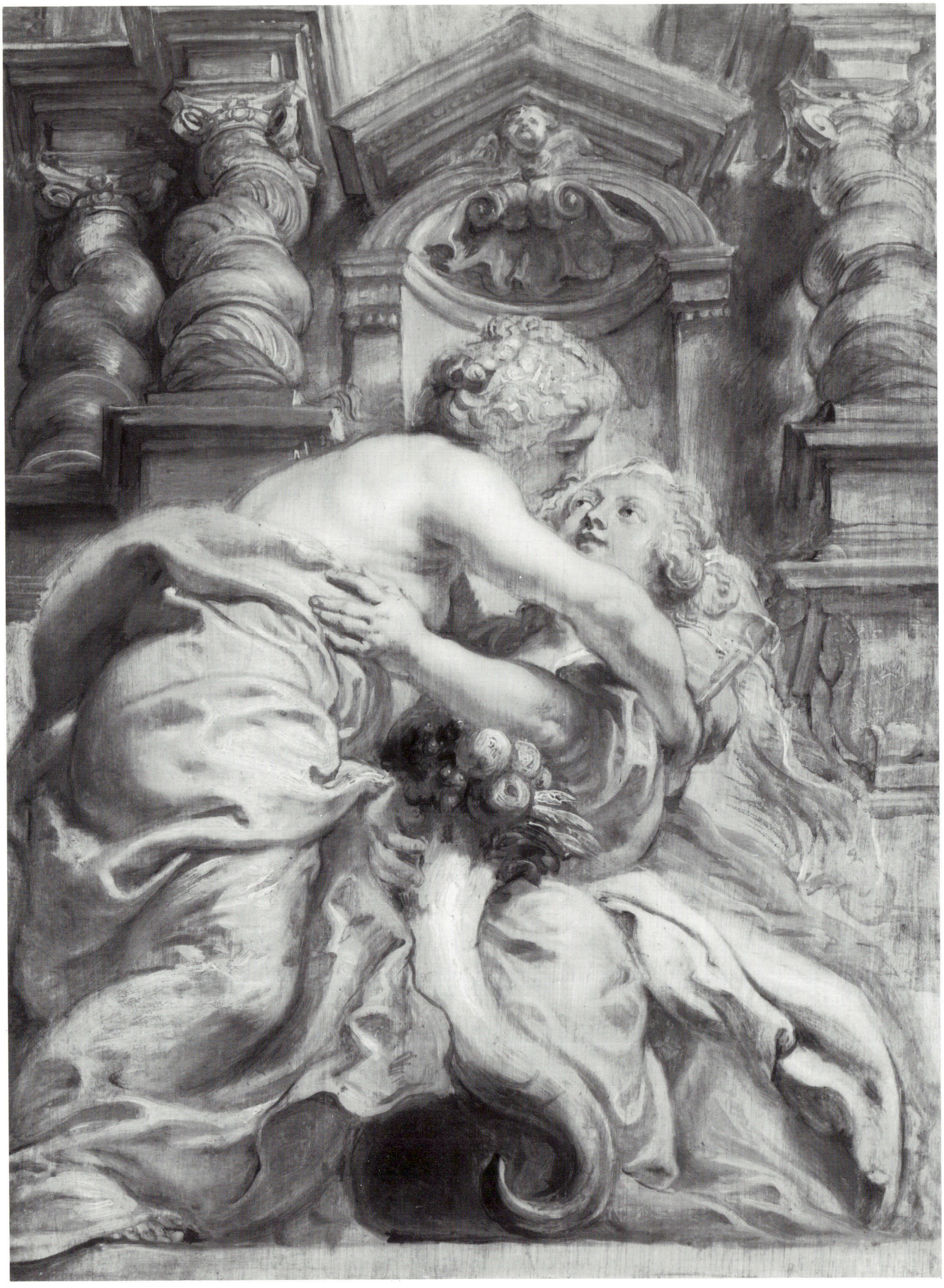

10. Sir Peter Paul Rubens, *Peace Embracing Plenty*, CAT. 48

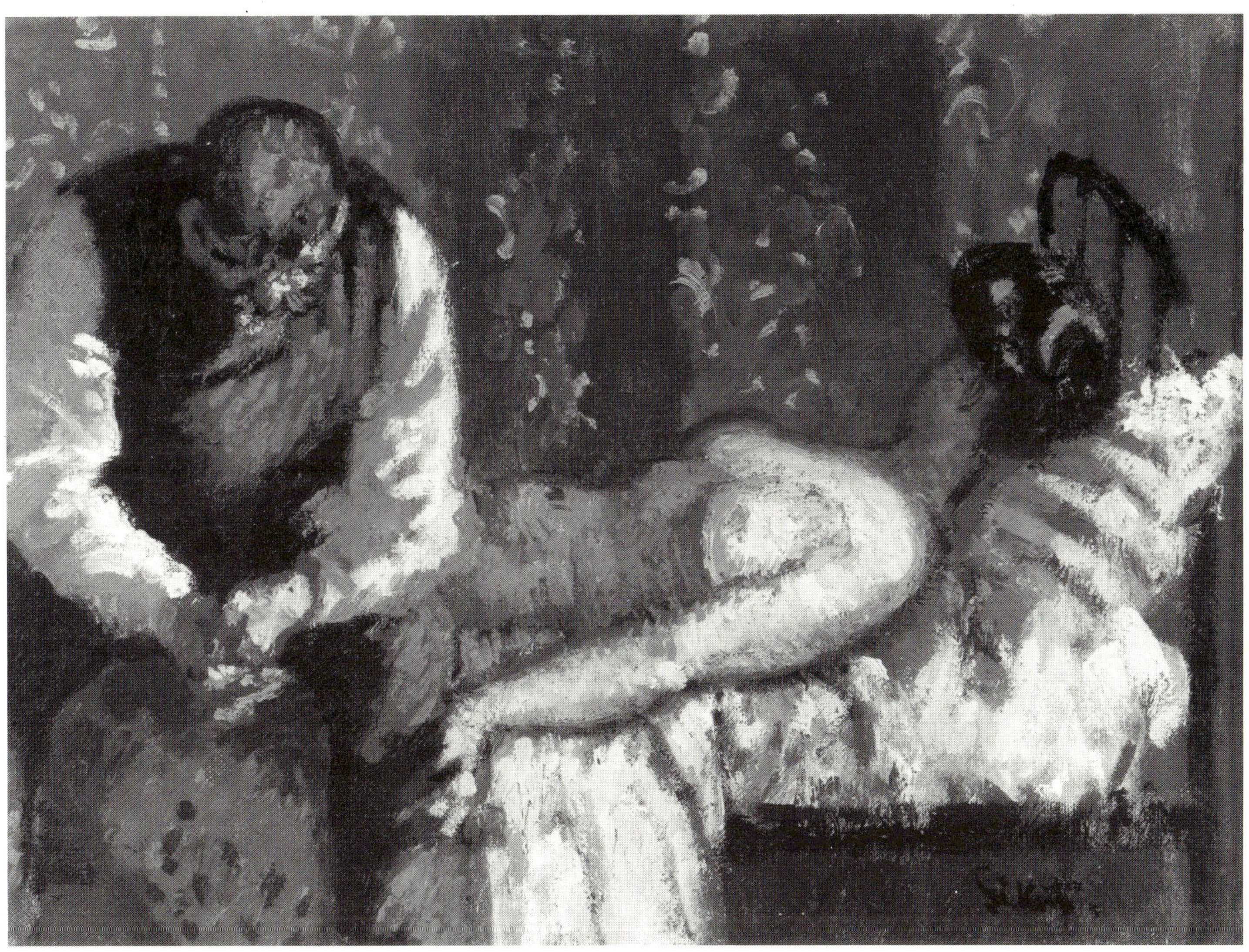

11. Walter Richard Sickert, *The Camden Town Murder, or What Shall We Do for the Rent?*, CAT. 51

48. SIR PETER PAUL RUBENS (1577-1640)

Peace Embracing Plenty, 1633-34

Oil on panel
$24\frac{3}{4} \times 18\frac{1}{2}$ in. (62.9 × 47.0 cm.)
Acquired Paul Mellon Fund 1977
B1977.14.70 **(Fig.10)**

49. PAUL SANDBY, R.A. (1730-1809)

Hackwood Park, Hampshire, signed, 1764

Oil on canvas
$40\frac{3}{16} \times 50\frac{1}{4}$ in. (102.1 × 127.6 cm.)
Acquired Paul Mellon Fund 1980
B1981.6

50. WALTER RICHARD SICKERT (1860-1942)

La Giuseppina, signed, c. 1903-04

Oil on canvas
$21\frac{1}{2} \times 18\frac{3}{16}$ in. (54.6 × 46.2 cm.)
Acquired Paul Mellon Fund 1979
B1979.37.2

51. WALTER RICHARD SICKERT (1860-1942)

The Camden Town Murder, or What Shall We Do for the Rent?, signed, c. 1908-09

Oil on canvas
$10\frac{1}{16} \times 14$ in. (25.6 × 35.5 cm.)
Acquired Paul Mellon Fund 1979
B1979.37.1 **(Fig.11)**

52. GEOFFREY ARTHUR TIBBLE (b. 1909)

Fitzroy Street (William Coldstream and Graham Bell in an Interior), 1938

Oil on canvas
27 × 32 in. (68.5 × 81.3 cm.)
Gift of Joseph F. McCrindle 1983
B1983.24.2

53. JOSEPH MALLORD WILLIAM TURNER (1775-1851)

Staffa, Fingal's Cave, 1832

Oil on canvas
$35\frac{3}{4} \times 47\frac{3}{4}$ in. (90.9 × 121.4 cm.)
Paul Mellon Collection 1978
B1978.43.14 **(Colour Fig.8. Page 6)**

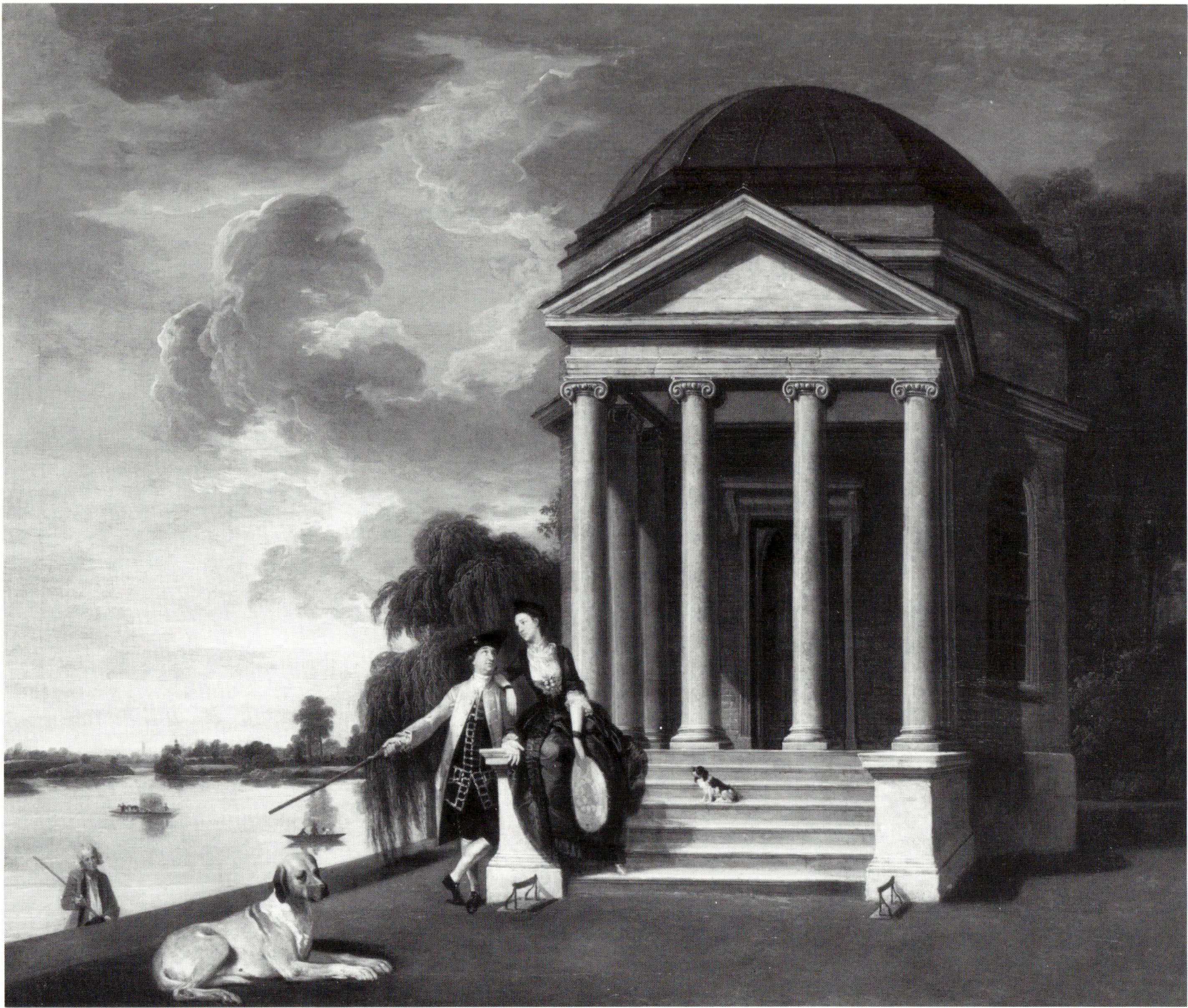

12. Johann Joseph Zoffany, R.A., *David Garrick and his Wife by his Temple to Shakespeare, at Hampton*, CAT. 59

54. JOSEPH MALLORD WILLIAM TURNER (1775-1851)

Wreckers – Coast of Northumberland, with a Steam Boat Assisting a Ship off Shore, 1834

Oil on canvas
$35\frac{5}{8} \times 47\frac{9}{16}$ in. (90.4 × 120.7 cm.)
Paul Mellon Collection 1978
B1978.43.15

55. JAMES WARD, R.A. (1769-1859)

A Hunter in a Landscape, signed and dated 1810

Oil on panel
$27\frac{7}{8} \times 35\frac{7}{8}$ in. (70.7 × 91.2 cm.)
Paul Mellon Collection 1977
B1978.43.18

56. BENJAMIN WEST, P.R.A. (1738-1820)

Isaac's Servant Tying the Bracelet on Rebecca's Arm,
signed and dated 1775

Oil on canvas
$49\frac{3}{4} \times 63\frac{3}{16}$ in. (126.4 × 160.5 cm.)
Paul Mellon Collection 1978
B1978.43.20

57. WILLEM WISSING (c. 1753/56-1687)

Elizabeth, Countess of Kildare, as a Shepherdess, c. 1684

Oil on canvas
$49\frac{1}{2} \times 39\frac{3}{4}$ in. (125.7 × 101.7 cm.)
Acquired Paul Mellon Fund 1984
B1984.19.1

58. JOHANN JOSEPH ZOFFANY, R.A. (1733-1810)

George, 3rd Earl Cowper, with the Family of Charles Gore,
c. 1775

Oil on canvas
$31 \times 38\frac{1}{2}$ in. (78.0 × 97.5 cm.)
Paul Mellon Collection 1977
B1977.14.87

59. JOHANN JOSEPH ZOFFANY, R.A. (1733-1810)

*David Garrick and his Wife by his Temple to Shakespeare,
at Hampton*, c. 1762

Oil on canvas
$43\frac{1}{4} \times 53$ in. (102.2 × 134.6 cm.)
Paul Mellon Collection 1981
B1981.25.737 **(Fig.12)**

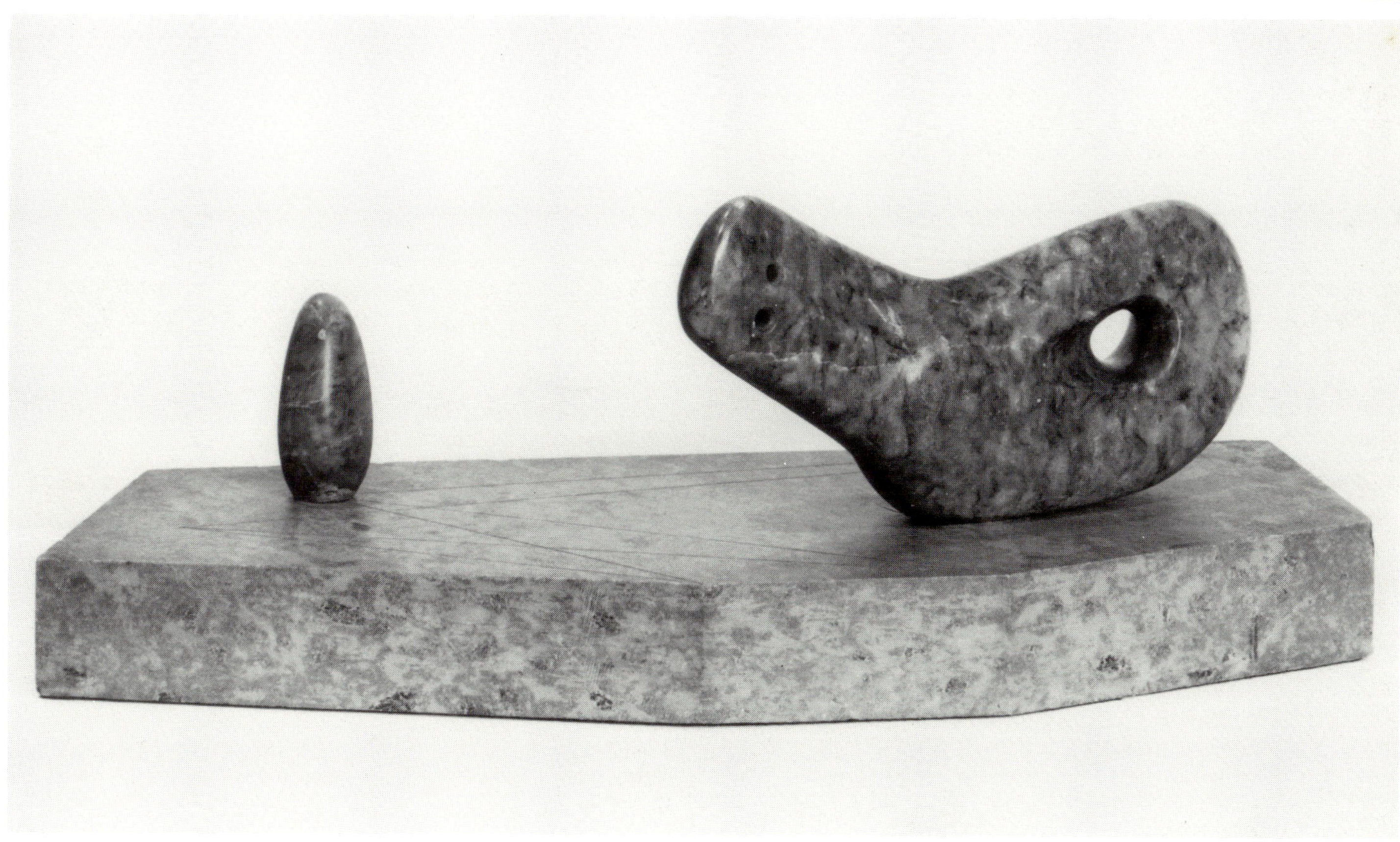

13. Henry Moore, O.M., *Bird and Egg*, CAT. 64

Sculpture

60. JOHN GIBSON, R.A. (1791-1866)

Aurora, signed, 1843-45

Marble
21 in. high (53.3 cm.)
Paul Mellon Collection 1978
B1978.5

61. JOHN GIBSON, R.A. (1791-1866)

William Roscoe (1753-1831), signed and dated 1819

Marble
$21\frac{7}{8}$ in. high (55.5 cm.)
Acquired Paul Mellon Fund 1983
B1983.13

62. JOSEPH GOTT (1786-1860)

A Greek Boxer Waiting his Turn, c. 1838

Marble
23 in. high (58.4 cm.)
Acquired Paul Mellon Fund 1980
B1980.34

63. DAME BARBARA HEPWORTH (1903-1975)

Sphere with Inner Form, 1963

Bronze
31 in. high (78.7 cm.)
Paul Mellon Collection 1966
B1984.6.2

64. HENRY MOORE, O.M. (1898-1986)

Bird and Egg, 1934

Cumberland alabaster
22 in. (base length) (56 cm.)
Paul Mellon Collection 1966
B1984.6.3 **(Fig.13)**

65. HENRY MOORE, O.M. (1898-1986)

Helmet Head, No. 3, signed, 1960

Bronze on metal base
$13\frac{7}{8}$ in. high (35.3 cm.)
Paul Mellon Collection 1965
B1984.6.1

66. JOSEPH NOLLEKENS, R.A. (1737-1823)

Portrait of a Man, probably Lord Granville Leveson-Gower, 1st Earl Granville (1773-1846), signed and dated 1810

Marble
29 in. high (70.4 cm.)
Acquired Paul Mellon Fund 1983
B1983.12

67. JOSEPH WILTON, R.A. (1722-1803)

Omphale, c. 1763

Terracotta
$28\frac{5}{8}$ in. high (70.3 cm.)
Paul Mellon Collection 1977
B1977.14.34

PRINTS AND DRAWINGS

A decade ago, almost to the month of this publication, as the nearly 45,000 prints and drawings recently donated by Paul Mellon were being uncrated and accessioned, the Yale Center for British Art acquired its first two works of art on paper. Funds from a newly established acquisitions grant were used to obtain Dante Gabriel Rossetti's study for *Dante in Meditation*, while Paul Mellon redoubled his commitment to the new museum by purchasing John Frederick Lewis's masterpiece, *A Frank Encampment in the Desert of Mt Sinai*. John Ruskin wrote breathlessly of the Lewis in 1856: 'if it gets into good hands, and is safely kept, it will one day be among the things which men will come to England from far away to see . . .'. Although the ranks of the earnest, in America and England, have not swelled appreciably since that first enthusiastic reception, it remains, like the more intimate Rossetti, one of our most admired objects of study.

Since 1976, the Department of Prints and Drawings has purchased, or received as gifts from donors too numerous to list, but here acknowledged with gratitude, some 1,500 drawings, sketch books and prints. Mention must be made also of another 1,000 drawings, including 600 by or attributed to George Romney, transferred in 1979 to the Center from the University Art Gallery, and of over 1,200 sporting prints donated by Paul Mellon last year. An ambitious exhibition programme, which draws on the collection's resources but does not ignore the institution's mandate to investigate the entire history of British graphic art, often has predisposed the curators towards certain artists and types of drawings. For example, an exhibition in 1980 of the 'exhibition water-colour', a class of object generally shunned by scholars and private collectors, prompted the purchase of superb pictures by Frederick Walker, A.W. Hunt, Frederick Burton, and R.R. Reinagle, to cite only those artists who were not previously represented at Yale.

The appeal of the Mellon drawings collection has always been its rich reserves of water-colours by the leading practitioners of romantic landscape painting. These have been augmented, most notably by the addition of five J.M.W. Turner water-colours. The magnificent *Whiting Fishing, Margate* and the unfinished 1804 Swiss subject, *The Devil's Bridge* (Col. Fig.10), were purchased from private American collectors. The weaknesses of the collection in 1976 were primarily in the areas of figural drawings, especially neo-classical subjects, and of Victorian and modern art. Since the opening of the Center, twelve works by the Pre-Raphaelites and their immediate followers have been acquired. Among

these are several early sheets by Sir John Everett Millais, of which the *Dying Man* (Fig.18) is one of the masterworks of that movement. Artists like Frederick Lord Leighton, Sir Edward Poynter, Sir Lawrence Alma-Tadema and Aubrey Beardsley have made their début during this decade, as have Richard Parkes Bonington (Col. Fig.3) and Sir David Wilkie as masters of the figural water-colour. Eighteenth-century acquisitions have been fewer in number, but they include Thomas Rowlandson's *Place des Victoires* (Col. Fig.6), Henry Fuseli's well-known *Selling of Cupids* (Fig.15), an album of seventy-seven studies by Sir Joshua Reynolds, and the largest extant group of George Stubbs's drawings, the 125 sheets illustrating his *Comparative Anatomical Exposition*.

During the last five years, a special effort has been made to embrace the modern era. Foremost among the 200 post-Victorian works acquired are water-colours by David Bomberg, Stanley Spencer (Fig.21), and Wyndham Lewis (Col. Fig.14), thirty-five preparatory chalk and pencil drawings by Spencer Gore for his mural decorations at the Cabaret Theatre Club, and a representative selection of sixty-eight drawings by the sculptor Henri Gaudier-Brzeska. Private donors have been very generous in their gifts of prints by the more popular painter-etchers, thus allowing purchase funds to be reserved for works by printmakers like John Copley and William Larkins. These interesting printmakers, and others of their generation, having missed the initial surge of American enthusiasm for turn-of-the-century etchers, are represented only sparsely in American print cabinets.

In compiling such a report, there is always a risk of exaggerating one's good fortune. There have, of course, been many disappointments. Beautiful and important works have been pursued but eventually lost to some other deserving institution or equally passionate collector. The decade has also witnessed a dramatic inflation of prices, to the point where a British drawing of any quality is often more expensive than an oil painting or the choicest old-master engraving. This market condition, while gratifying in its proof of a serious public interest in British art, has gradually decreased the number of our annual purchases. But our unremitting effort to expand and to refine the collections, and ultimately to enrich the studies of students, scholars and amateurs alike, is all the more satisfying for these challenges. We can only hope that the next decade of collecting will be as interesting and as bountiful.

PATRICK NOON
Curator of Prints and Drawings

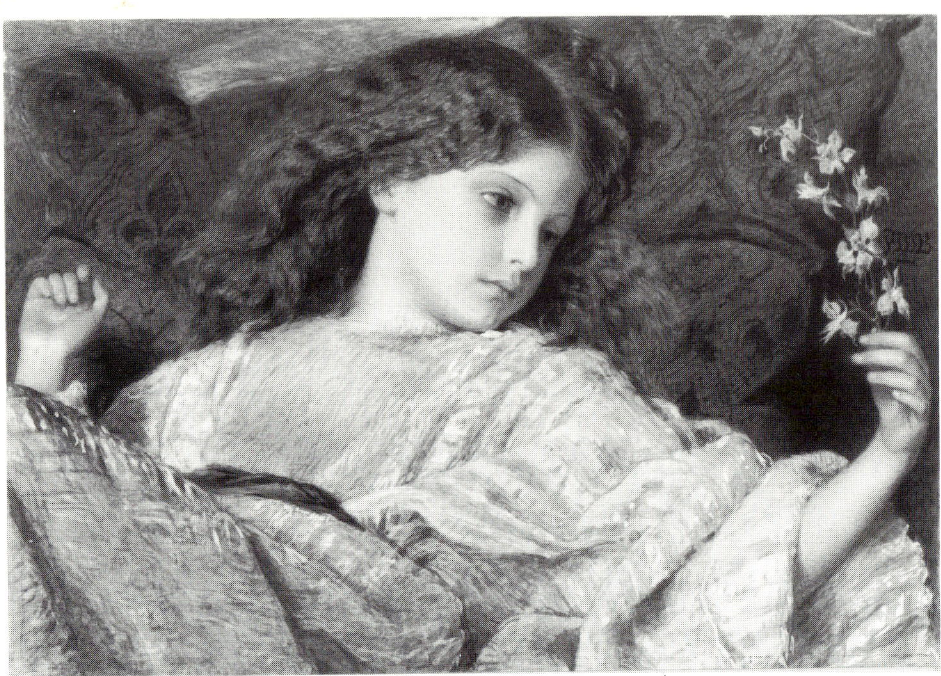

14. Sir Frederick William Burton, *Dreams*, CAT. 75

68. HELEN ALLINGHAM (1848-1926)

Last House at Lynmouth, Northumberland, 1874

Water-colour and body-colour on heavy wove paper
$7\frac{1}{2} \times 10\frac{7}{16}$ in. (19 × 26.5 cm.)
Signed and dated: H. Allingham/74

Acquired Paul Mellon Fund 1986
B1986.4

69. FRANK AUERBACH (b. 1931)

Head of Christopher Dark, II, 1977

Black chalk and charcoal on heavy wove paper
$30 \times 22\frac{1}{2}$ in. (76.2 × 57.2 cm.)

Gift of R.B. Kitaj 1982
B1982.15.24

70. GEORGE BARRET, JUNIOR (1767-1842)

Tivoli – Classical Composition, c. 1820-30

Water-colour over pencil, with white body-colour and scratching out on
wove paper
$27\frac{7}{8} \times 40\frac{3}{16}$ in. (70.8 × 102 cm.)

Acquired Paul Mellon Fund 1984
B1984.24.1

71. AUBREY BEARDSLEY (1872-1898)

A Large Christmas Card, 1895

Pen and black ink over pencil on wove paper
$9\frac{5}{8} \times 6\frac{1}{4}$ in. (24.4 × 15.8 cm.)
Signed: Aubrey Beardsley

Acquired Paul Mellon Fund 1979
B1979.1.1

72. DAVID BOMBERG (1890-1957)

Study for 'Reading the Torah', c. 1914

Water-colour and body-colour over pencil on wove paper
verso: pencil
image: $8\frac{1}{8} \times 8\frac{3}{4}$ in. (20.7 × 22.2 cm.)
sheet: $10 \times 12\frac{7}{8}$ in. (25.5 × 32.7 cm.)
Signed: David Bomberg

Acquired Paul Mellon Fund 1984
B1984.27.2

73. RICHARD PARKES BONINGTON (1802-1828)

The Present, c. 1826

Water-colour, brown ink, and body-colour with scraping out over pencil
on wove paper
$6\frac{1}{2} \times 5\frac{1}{16}$ in. (16.5 × 12.8 cm.)
Signed: R P Bonington

Paul Mellon Collection 1978
B1978.43.165   **(Colour Fig.3. Page 4)**

74. SIR EDWARD COLEY BURNE-JONES (1833-1898)

The Land of Beulah, 1881

Pen and brown and black ink over pencil on wove paper
$8 \times 11\frac{3}{8}$ in. (20.3 × 29.8 cm.)
Inscribed: LG from EBT [monogram]/July 18 1881;
and quotation from *Pilgrim's Progress*

Acquired Paul Mellon Fund 1978
B1978.36.1

75. SIR FREDERICK WILLIAM BURTON (1816-1900)

Dreams, 1861

Water-colour, body-colour and gum over pencil on wove paper
8×12 in. (20.3 × 30.6 cm.)
Signed in monogram: F W B

Acquired Paul Mellon Fund 1980
B1980.37   **(Fig.14)**

76. JOHN COPLEY (1875-1950)

Tennis Players, 1918

Lithograph on laid paper
$9 \times 6\frac{3}{4}$ in. (22.9 × 17.2 cm.)

Acquired Paul Mellon Fund 1985
B1985.29.1

77. JOHN SELL COTMAN (1782-1842)

Mountainous Landscape, North Wales, c. 1802

Water-colour touched with gum over pencil on heavy wove paper
$8\frac{1}{2} \times 12\frac{3}{4}$ in. (21.5 × 32.4 cm.)

Acquired Paul Mellon Fund 1982
B1982.11.2

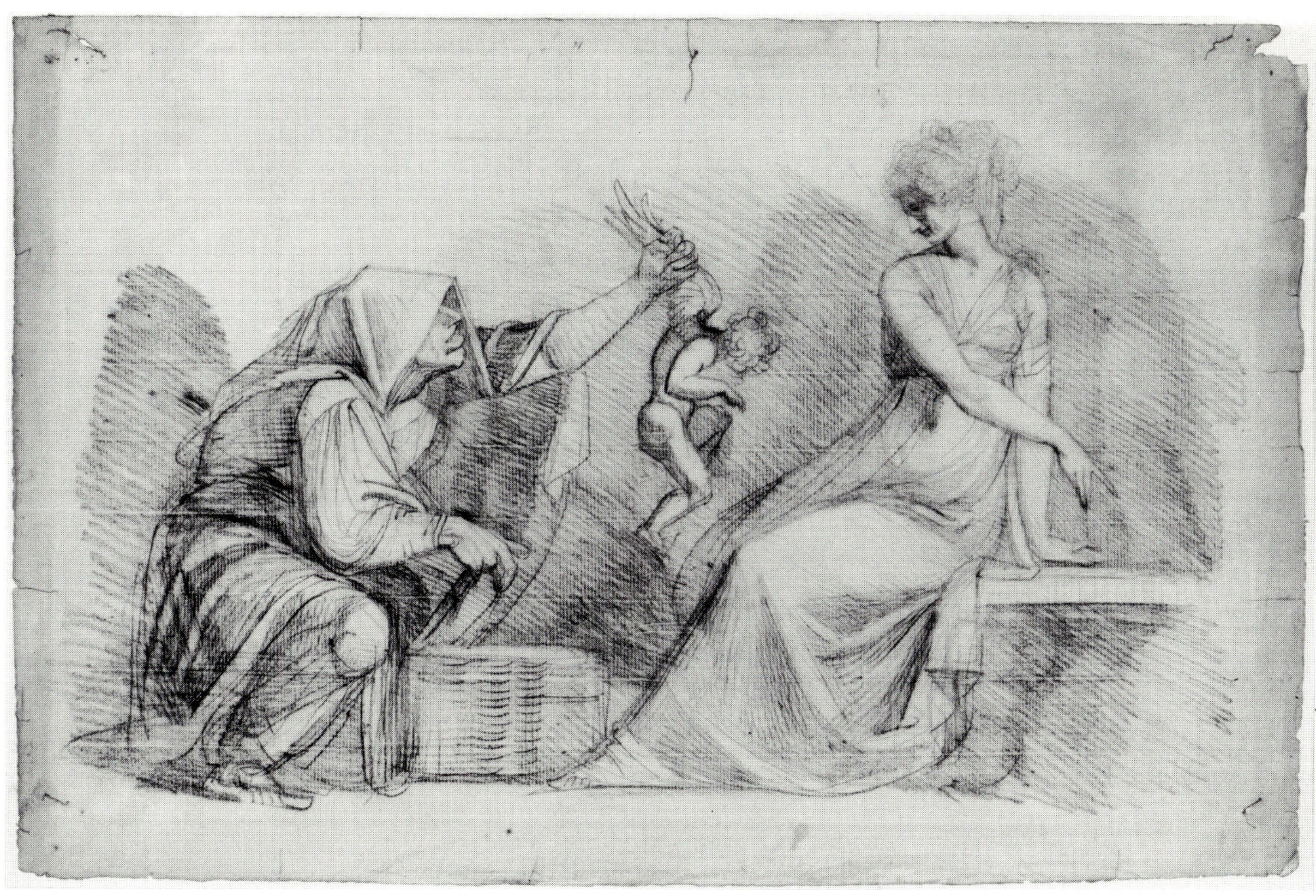

15. Henry Fuseli, R.A., *Selling of Cupids*, CAT. 84

78. DAVID COX (1783-1859)

Windermere during the Regatta, 1832

Water-colour and body-colour over pencil with gum and scratching out
on wove paper
$17\frac{3}{4} \times 24$ in. (45.1 × 61 cm.)
Signed and dated: D. Cox. 1832

Acquired Paul Mellon Fund 1985
B1985.24   **(Colour Fig.9. Page 6)**

79. ALEXANDER COZENS (1717-1786)

St Peter's from the Villa Barberini, 1746

Pencil on laid paper
$5 \times 7\frac{1}{4}$ in. (12.7 × 18.5 cm.)
B1978.43.166z verso

This drawing appears on p. 44 verso of Cozens's *Roman Sketchbook*
(B1978.43.166 a-hhh), Paul Mellon Collection 1978

80. JOHN ROBERT COZENS (1772-1799)

Willow, 1789

Soft ground etching on pale yellow hand-tinted wove paper
$9\frac{3}{8} \times 12\frac{3}{8}$ in. (23.9 × 31.5 cm.)
Inscribed: Willow
B1985.13.12

One of fourteen soft ground etchings from *Studies of Trees*
(B1985.13.1-14), acquired Paul Mellon Fund 1985

81. FRANCIS DANBY (1793-1861)

A Midsummer Night's Dream, 1837

Water-colour and body-colour with gum over pencil on wove paper
$6 \times 8\frac{1}{4}$ in. (15.3 × 20.9 cm.)

Acquired Paul Mellon Fund 1978
B1978.2.1

82. FRANÇOIS LOUIS THOMAS FRANCIA (1772-1839)

Pont de la Concorde from the Cours La Reine, 1823

Water-colour with scraping out over pencil on wove paper
$6\frac{5}{8} \times 10\frac{5}{8}$ in. (16.8 × 27 cm.)
Signed and dated: L Francia/1823

Acquired Paul Mellon Fund 1985
B1985.11.2

83. GEORGE ARTHUR FRIPP (1813-1896)

Durham Cathedral, 1840

Water-colour with body-colour and scratching out over pencil on heavy
wove paper
$14\frac{3}{16} \times 24\frac{13}{16}$ in. (36 × 63 cm.)
Signed and dated: G.A. Fripp/1840

Acquired Paul Mellon Fund 1984
B1984.24.2

84. HENRY FUSELI (1741-1825)

Selling of Cupids, c. 1775-76

Black and red chalk and pencil on laid paper
$12\frac{1}{4} \times 19\frac{1}{16}$ in. (31.1 × 48.4 cm.)

Acquired Paul Mellon Fund 1982
B1982.8   **(Fig.15)**

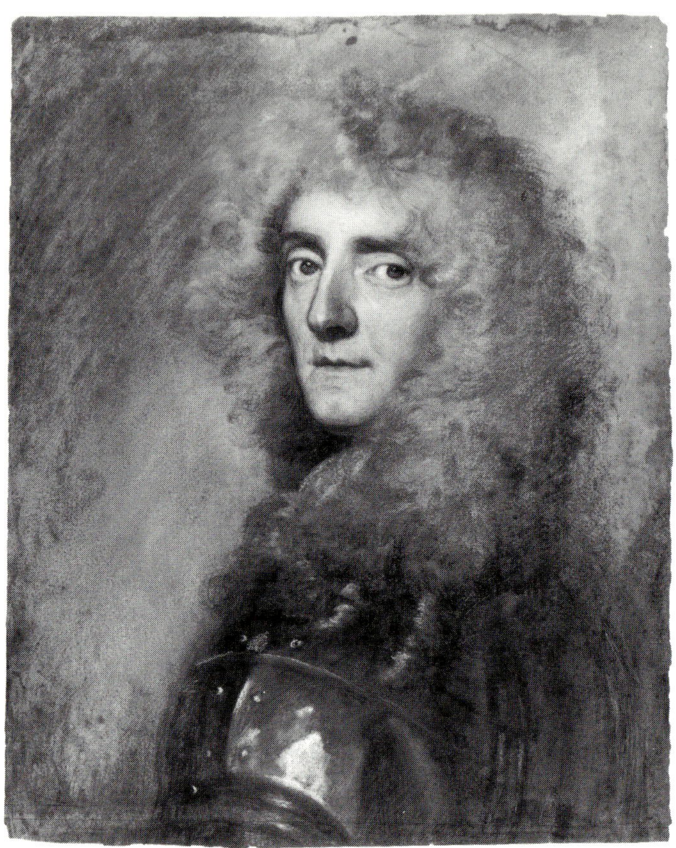

16. John Greenhill, *Portrait of Philip Woolrich*, CAT. 90

85. HENRI GAUDIER-BRZESKA (1891-1915)

Portrait of Katharine Mansfield, c. 1912-13

Black chalk on wove paper
$14\frac{1}{4} \times 10\frac{1}{8}$ in. (36.3 × 25.8 cm.)
Inscribed: à K.M./Hgaudierbrzeska
B1982.26.60

From an album containing sixty-eight drawings by Gaudier-Brzeska (B1982.26.1-68), acquired Paul Mellon Fund 1982

86. ERIC GILL (1882-1940)

Design for Bas-Relief of Calf in the Cave of the Golden Calf, c. 1912

Water-colour and pencil on wove paper, squared for transfer in pencil
$9\frac{5}{16} \times 15\frac{3}{4}$ in. (23.7 × 40 cm.)
Acquired Paul Mellon Fund 1985
B1985.25.9

87. SPENCER FREDERICK GORE (1878-1914)

Study for Deer-Hunting Mural in the Cave of the Golden Calf, c. 1912

Crayon and pencil on wove paper
10×14 in. (25.4 × 25.6 cm.)
Acquired Paul Mellon Fund 1985
B1985.25.2

88. SYLVIA GOSSE (1881-1968)

Woman in Bed, c. 1920

Black crayon on light blue wove paper
$11\frac{3}{16} \times 9\frac{1}{8}$ in. (28.4 × 23.2 cm.)
Signed: Gosse

Acquired Paul Mellon Fund 1979
B1979.31.3

89. JOSEPH GOUPY (c. 1680-1763)
     after RAPHAEL (1483-1520)

Death of Ananias, 1740

Body-colour over pencil on parchment
$11\frac{7}{8} \times 18$ in. (30.2 × 45.7 cm.)
Signed: Jo. Goupy

Acquired Paul Mellon Fund 1986
B1986.13
Original frame, carved and gilt wood by Paul Petit, 1740

90. JOHN GREENHILL (1604/5-1676)

Portrait of Philip Woolrich, c. 1676

Pastel and black chalk on laid paper
$12\frac{3}{4} \times 10\frac{1}{2}$ in. (31.9 × 26.7 cm.)

Acquired Paul Mellon Fund 1978
B1978.3.4 **(Fig.16)**

91. GAVIN HAMILTON (1723-1798)

Classical Composition

Pen and brush and grey ink over pencil on laid paper
$13\frac{1}{8} \times 17\frac{11}{16}$ in. (33.3 × 44.9 cm.)

Acquired Paul Mellon Fund 1978
B1978.11.2

92. BENJAMIN ROBERT HAYDON (1786-1849)

Portrait of a Gentleman, c. 1835

Black and white chalk on brown wove paper
$22 \times 17\frac{3}{8}$ in. (55.9 × 44.1 cm.)
Inscribed: never paid/ BR Haydon/W Winston [illeg]

Acquired Paul Mellon Fund 1980
B1980.38.2

93. WILLIAM HOARE (1707-1792)

Alexander Pope, after 1739-40

Pastel on wove paper
$23 \times 16\frac{3}{4}$ in. (58.5 × 42.6 cm.)

Gift of Maynard Mack 1986
B1986.21

94. ALFRED WILLIAM HUNT (1830-1896)

'Blue Lights', Tynemouth Pier – Lighting the Lamps at Sundown, 1868

Water-colour, body-colour, gum and scraping out
$14\frac{5}{8} \times 21\frac{1}{4}$ in. (37.2 × 54 cm.)
Signed and dated: A W Hunt, 1868

Acquired Paul Mellon Fund 1980
B1980.3 **(Colour Fig.11. Page 7)**

95. AUGUSTUS JOHN (1878-1961)

Self-Portrait, c. 1897

Red chalk on wove paper
$12\frac{7}{8} \times 9\frac{3}{4}$ in. (33.1 × 25.6 cm.)
Signed: John

Acquired Paul Mellon Fund 1978
B1978.23

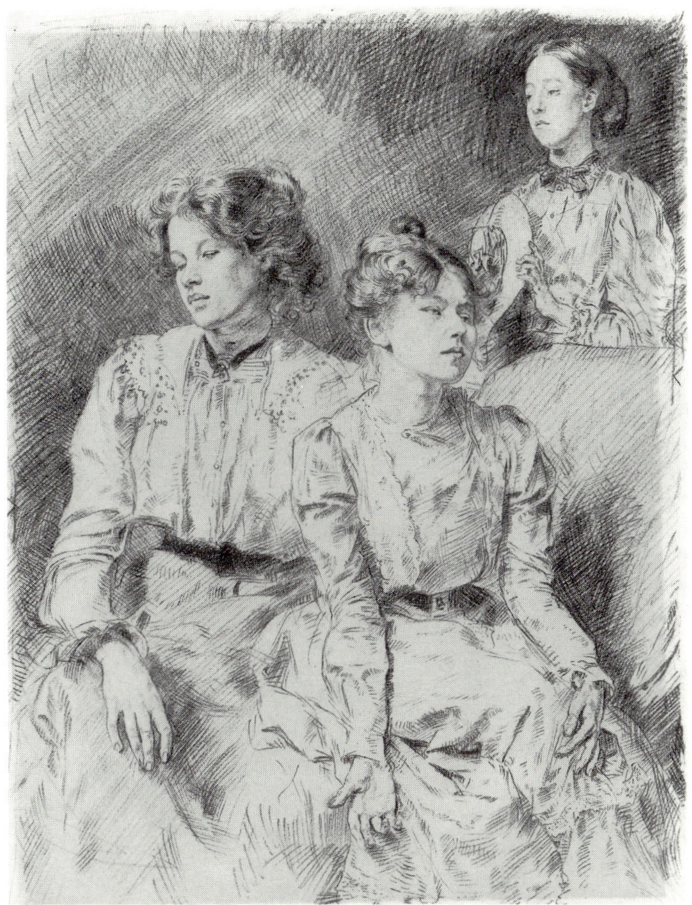

17. Augustus John, R.A., *Portrait of Gwen John, Ida Nettleship and Ursula Tyrwhitt*, CAT. 96

96. AUGUSTUS JOHN (1878-1961)

Portrait of Gwen John, Ida Nettleship and Ursula Tyrwhitt,
c. 1899

Pencil on wove paper
13 × 9⅞ in. (33 × 25 cm.)
Gift of Paul Mellon 1985
B1985.19.7 **(Fig.17)**

97. R. B. KITAJ (b. 1932)

Madame Jane Junk and Joe, 1970

Screenprint, No. 28 from an edition of 70
27⅝ × 40 in. (70.2 × 101.7 cm.)
Signed and numbered: Kitaj 28/70
Anonymous Gift 1983
B1983.31.13

98. SIR THOMAS LAWRENCE (1769-1830)

Portrait of a Lady, thought to be Elizabeth Lysons, 1795

Pencil and red chalk on wove paper
10 × 7¹³⁄₁₆ in. (25.4 × 19.8 cm.)
Signed with monogram and dated: T.L./1795
Acquired Paul Mellon Fund 1985
B1985.15.3

99. FREDERICK LEIGHTON, LORD LEIGHTON OF STRETTON (1830-1896)

Study for 'Solitude', c. 1890

Black and white chalk on brown wove paper
14½ × 11¼ in. (36.8 × 28.5 cm.)
Inscribed: Solitude
Acquired Paul Mellon Fund 1985
B1985.5

100. BERNARD LENS III (1682-1740)
after SIR PETER PAUL RUBENS (1577-1640)

Mars Introduced by Minerva to Occasion, Accompanied by Ceres,
1720

Body-colour and gum on vellum
15½ × 18¾ in. (39.4 × 47.6 cm.)
Signed and dated: B. Lens Fecit./July 21: 1720
Acquired Paul Mellon Fund 1982
B1982.6

101. BERNARD LENS III (1682-1740)

Classical Landscape, 1717

Body-colour and gum over pencil on vellum
7¹¹⁄₁₆ × 10¼ in. (19.5 × 26 cm.)
Signed and dated: B. Lens Fecit 1717
Acquired Paul Mellon Fund 1985
B1985.11.1

102. JOHN FREDERICK LEWIS (1805-1876)

A Frank Encampment in the Desert at Mount Sinai, 1842, 1856

Water-colour and body-colour with gum over pencil on beige wove
paper
25½ × 52⅞ in. (64.8 × 134.3 cm.)
Signed and dated: J. F. Lewis/1856
Gift of Paul Mellon 1977
B1977.14.143

103. JOHN FREDERICK LEWIS (1805-1876)

Study for 'The Proclamation of Don Carlos', c. 1834-38

Water-colour, body-colour, with scraping out over black chalk and pencil
on two joined sheets of heavy wove paper
7½ × 10⁷⁄₁₆ in. (44.5 × 26.5 cm.)
Acquired Paul Mellon Fund 1980
B1980.22.1

104. WYNDHAM LEWIS (1882-1957)

Kermesse, 1912

Body-colour and water-colour with pen and black ink over pencil on
two joined sheets of wove paper
12 × 12¹⁄₁₆ in. (30.5 × 35.1 cm.)
Signed and dated: Wyndham Lewis/1912
Acquired Paul Mellon Fund and Gift of Neil F. and Ivan E. Phillips in
memory of their mother, Mrs. Rosalie Phillips 1982
B1982.1 **(Colour Fig.14. Page 8)**

105. WYNDHAM LEWIS (1882-1957)

Abstract Figure Study, 1921

Pen and black ink and white body-colour on wove paper
10⅜ × 6¾ in. (26.4 × 17.2 cm.)
Signed with monogram and dated: W.L./1921
Acquired Paul Mellon Fund 1985
B1985.30

106. SIR JOHN EVERETT MILLAIS (1829-1896)

Study for 'The Woodman's Daughter', 1849

Pen and black ink, grey wash, and scraping out over pencil on tan wove
paper
7 × 4¹⁵⁄₁₆ in. (17.8 × 12.6 cm.)
Signed and dated: J.E. Millais/1849
Acquired Paul Mellon Fund 1979
B1979.23

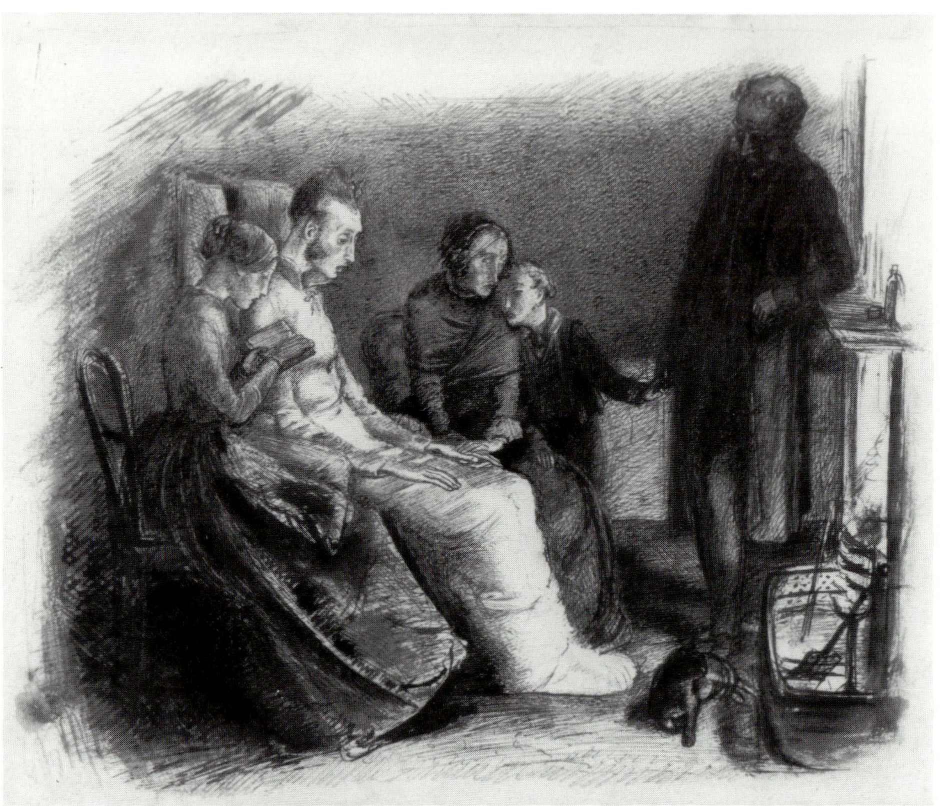

18. Sir John Everett Millais, P.R.A., *The Dying Man*, CAT. 107

107. SIR JOHN EVERETT MILLAIS (1829-1896)

The Dying Man, c. 1853-1854

Pen and brown ink, brown wash, and brown chalk on wove paper
7¾ × 9⅝ in. (19.7 × 24.5 cm.)
Acquired Paul Mellon Fund 1979
B1979.24 **(Fig.18)**

108. SIR JOHN EVERETT MILLAIS (1829-1896)

The Blind Man, 1853

Pen and brown ink, brown wash, and pencil on wove paper
8 × 10¾ in. (20.3 × 27.3 cm.)
Signed in monogram and dated: J E M/1853
Acquired Paul Mellon Fund 1980
B1980.12

109. SIR JOHN EVERETT MILLAIS (1829-1896)

Study for the Head of Ferdinand in 'Ferdinand Lured by Ariel',
1849

Pencil on wove paper
6¹³⁄₁₆ × 5¹⁄₁₆ in. (17.3 × 12.9 cm.)
Signed and dated: J E Millais 1849
Acquired Paul Mellon Fund 1980
B1980.25.2

110. ALBERT MOORE (1841-1893)

Study for 'Battledore and Shuttlecock', c. 1871

Black and white chalk over pencil on brown wove paper
image: 6⅝ × 11¾ in. (16 × 29.9 cm.)
sheet: 9¼ × 14½ in. (23.5 × 36.8 cm.)
Acquired Paul Mellon Fund 1984
B1984.1.1

111. CHARLES FAIRFAX MURRAY (1849-1919)

Portrait Study of a Woman

Water-colour over pencil on wove paper
13¹⁵⁄₁₆ × 10 in. (35.4 × 25.3 cm.)
Acquired Paul Mellon Fund 1979
B1979.13

112. PAUL NASH (1889-1946)

A Shell Crater, 1918

Coloured chalks on dark brown paper
10 × 14 in. (25.4 × 35.6 cm.)
Signed: Paul Nash
Acquired Paul Mellon Fund 1978
B1978.36.3

113. PAUL NASH (1889-1946)

Winter, Hampden, 1921

Woodcut on wove paper
Trimmed within the plate mark: 6½ × 29½ in. (16.5 × 11.5 cm.)
Inscribed: To John for Christmas/Winter/Paul Nash/1921
Acquired Paul Mellon Fund 1985
B1985.6.2

114. JOSEPH PENNELL (1860-1926)

Rainy Night, Charing Cross Station, 1886

Etching on laid paper
plate: 6¹⁵⁄₁₆ × 8¹⁵⁄₁₆ in. (17.7 × 22.7 cm.)
sheet: 9¹⁄₁₆ × 11¼ in. (23.1 × 28.6 cm.)
Signed: J Pennell; and inscribed: Charing Cross Underground
night/Goulding imp.
Gift of Daniel Bell 1985
B1985.31.10

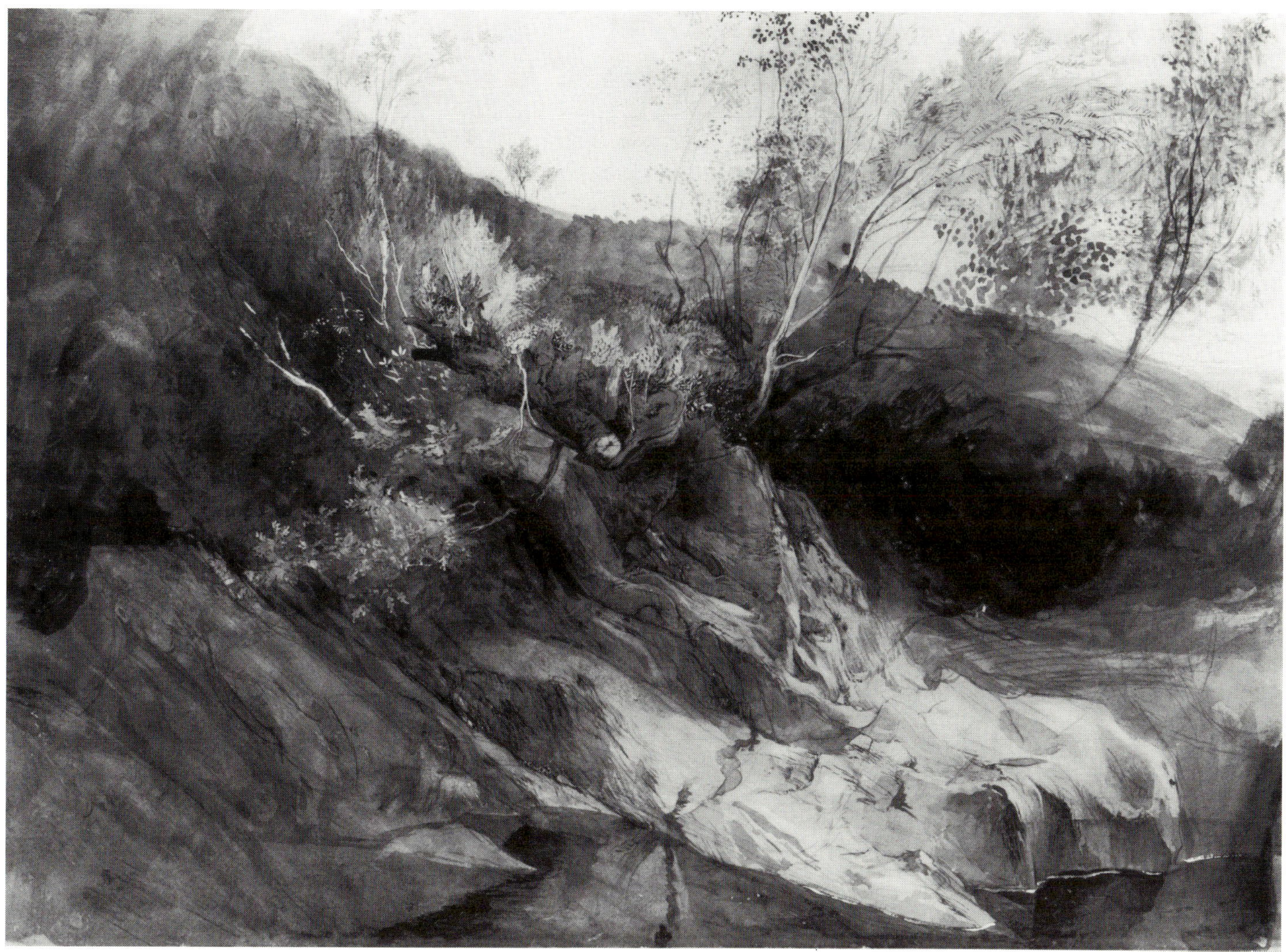

19. John Ruskin, *Rocky Bank of a River*, CAT. 119

115. SIR EDWARD JOHN POYNTER (1836-1919)

Landscape Near Ageles-Gazost at the Foot of the Pyrenees

Water-colour on wove paper
$5\frac{1}{2} \times 8\frac{5}{16}$ in. (13.9 × 21.1 cm.)
Signed in monogram: E J P

Acquired Paul Mellon Fund 1978
B1978.2.4

116a. SIR JOSHUA REYNOLDS (1723-1792)

Study of a Seated Shepherd

Pencil on laid paper
$5\frac{1}{4} \times 8\frac{3}{4}$ in. (13.4 × 22.2 cm.)
B1982.24.15

116b. *Study for an Equestrian Portrait of George IV, when
       Prince of Wales*, c. 1784

Pen and brown ink and pencil on laid paper
$9 \times 7\frac{3}{16}$ in. (22.9 × 18.3 cm.)
B1982.24.16

From an album of seventy-seven drawings by Reynolds
(B1982.24.1-78), acquired Paul Mellon Fund 1982

117. DANTE GABRIEL ROSSETTI (1828-1882)

Dante in Meditation Holding a Pomegranate, c.1852

Pen and black ink and pencil on wove paper
$9\frac{5}{16} \times 7\frac{13}{16}$ in. (23.7 × 19.8 cm.)
Signed in monogram: D G R

Acquired Paul Mellon Fund 1976
B1976.3

118. THOMAS ROWLANDSON (1756-1827)

Place des Victoires, c. 1789

Water-colour, pen and black ink over pencil on laid paper
$13\frac{15}{16} \times 21$ in. (38 × 53.4 cm.)

Acquired Paul Mellon Fund 1981
B1981.7   **(Colour Fig.6. Page 5)**

119. JOHN RUSKIN (1819-1900)

Rocky Bank of a River, c. 1853

verso: Study of foliage
Grey wash with pen and black ink over pencil heightened with white
body-colour on heavy wove paper
verso: pen and brown ink over pencil
$12\frac{7}{8} \times 18\frac{5}{8}$ in. (32.7 × 47.4 cm.)

Acquired Paul Mellon Fund 1984
B1984.13   **(Fig.19)**

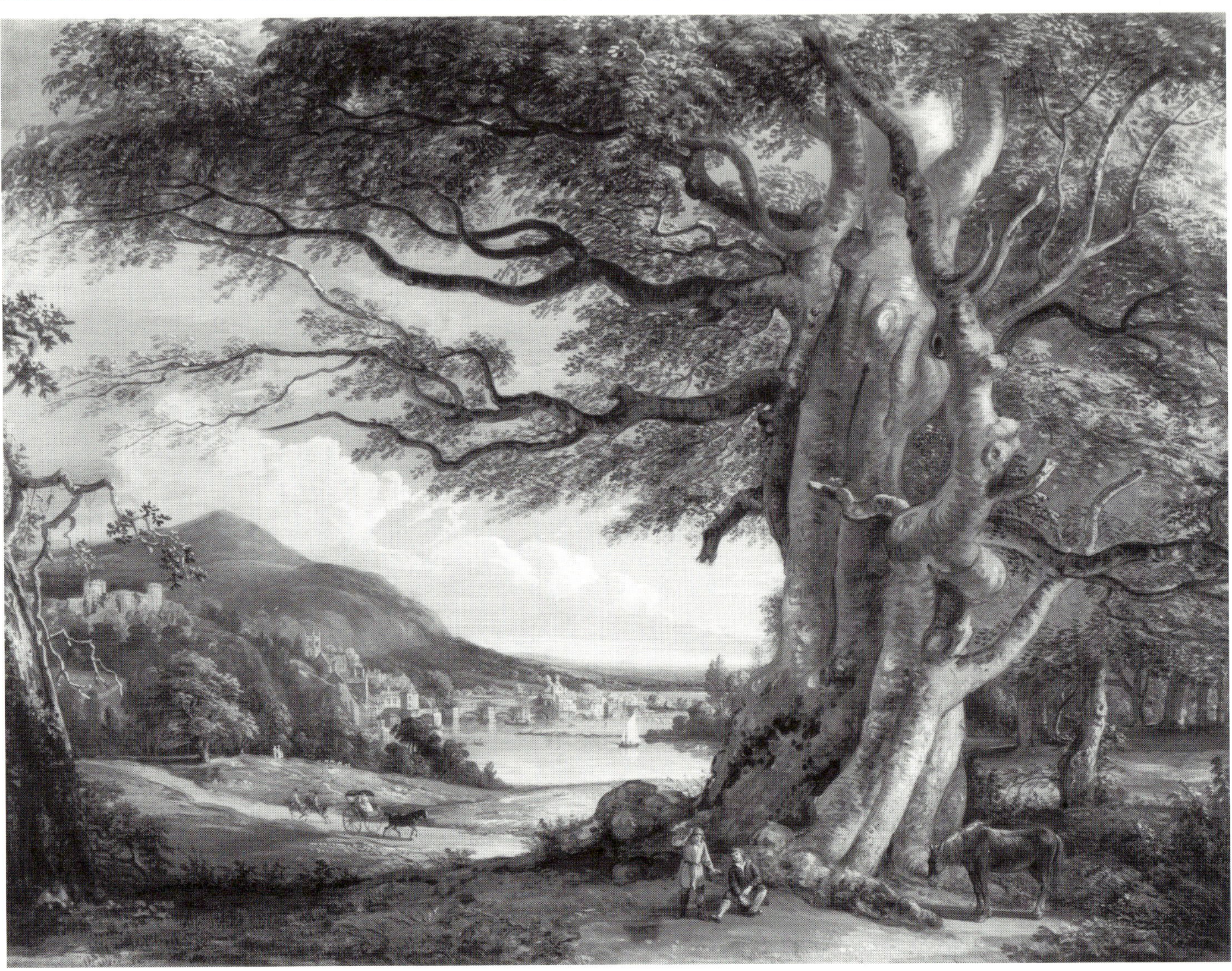

20. Paul Sandby, R.A., *Bridgenorth, Shropshire*, CAT. 121

120. JOHN RUSSELL (1745-1806)

Head of a Man, c. 1785

Pastel on heavy wove paper
$13\frac{1}{2} \times 10\frac{7}{16}$ in. (34.2 × 26.4 cm.)
Gift of Robert H. Wexler, Class of 1950, in honour of Jerrold A. Wexler, Class of 1953, 1979
B1979.27

121. PAUL SANDBY (1730-1809)

Bridgenorth, Shropshire, c. 1801

Water-colour and body-colour over black chalk and pencil on wove paper
$26 \times 35\frac{1}{2}$ in. (66 × 90.2 cm.)
Acquired Paul Mellon Fund 1983
B1983.9.1   **(Fig.20)**

122. GILBERT SPENCER (1892-1928)

Self-Portrait, c. 1913-14

Pencil on two joined sheets of wove paper
$14\frac{1}{2} \times 8\frac{11}{16}$ in. (36.8 × 22.1 cm.)
Signed: Gilbert Spencer
Acquired Paul Mellon Fund 1984
B1984.1.2

123. SIR STANLEY SPENCER (1891-1959)

Deposition, 1910

Brown wash with pen and black ink and pencil on wove paper
sheet: $14\frac{3}{8} \times 9\frac{7}{8}$ in. (36.5 × 25 cm.)
Signed and dated: S Spencer/1910
Acquired Paul Mellon Fund 1984
B1984.27.1   **(Fig.21)**

124. GEORGE STUBBS (1724-1806)

Tiger, Lateral View, with Skin and Tissue Removed, c. 1795-1804

Pencil on heavy wove paper
$16\frac{1}{8} \times 21\frac{1}{8}$ in. (41.1 × 53.7 cm.)
B1980.1.9

This is one of 125 surviving drawings for Stubbs's *A Comparative Anatomical Exposition of the Structure of the Human Body with That of a Tiger and a Common Fowl*, acquired Paul Mellon Fund 1980.

125. GRAHAM SUTHERLAND (1903-1980)

Pecken Wood, 1925

Etching on wove paper
plate: $5\frac{1}{2} \times 7\frac{7}{16}$ in. (13.9 × 18.9 cm.)
sheet: $9\frac{3}{16} \times 11\frac{3}{16}$ in. (23.3 × 28.4 cm.)
Signed and dated within the plate mark: Graham Sutherland MCMXXV.+; signed and dated: Graham Sutherland MCMXXV.+; and inscribed: P.W. a.5.imp.
Acquired Paul Mellon Fund 1984
B1984.5.3

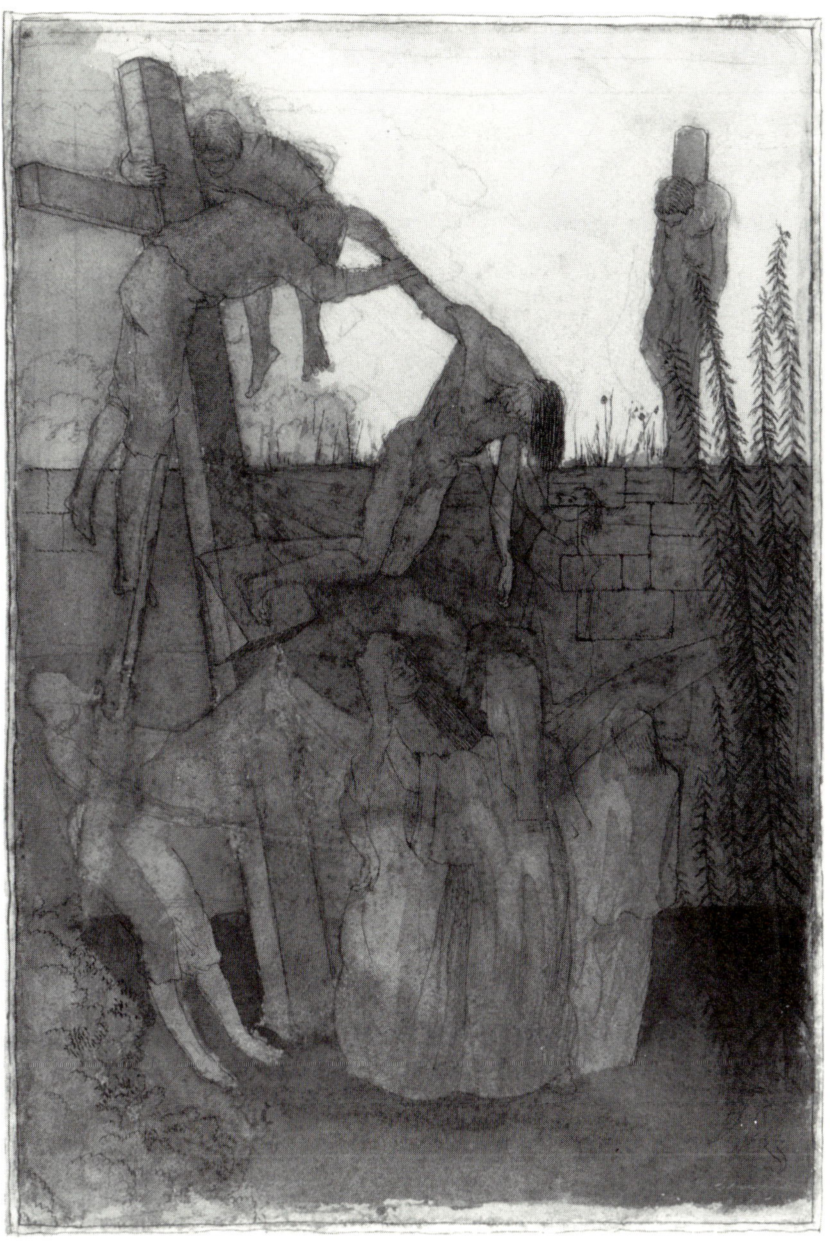

21. Sir Stanley Spencer, *Deposition*, CAT. 123

126. FRANCIS TOWNE (1740-1816)

The Claudian Aqueduct, Rome, 1785

Water-colour with pen and black ink over pencil on laid paper
$12\frac{5}{8} \times 18\frac{9}{16}$ in. (32.1 × 47.1 cm.)
Signed and dated: F. Towne delt./1785

Paul Mellon Collection 1978
B1978.43.170

127. JOSEPH MALLORD WILLIAM TURNER (1775-1851)

The Devil's Bridge, c. 1803-04

Water-colour, white wax crayon, and scraping out on wove paper
$41\frac{11}{16} \times 29\frac{7}{8}$ in. (105.9 × 75.9 cm.)
Acquired Paul Mellon Fund 1981
B1981.12   **(Colour Fig.10. Page 7)**

128. WILLIAM TURNER OF OXFORD (1789-1862)

Scene near Shipton-on-Cherwell, Oxfordshire, 1835

Water-colour, body-colour, and gum over pencil with scraping out on
wove paper
$21\frac{9}{16} \times 29\frac{5}{8}$ in. (54.7 × 75.2 cm.)
Acquired Paul Mellon Fund 1981
B1981.24

129. FREDERICK WALKER (1840-1875)

Strange Faces, 1863

Water-colour and body-colour over white ground with gum on wove
paper
$25\frac{15}{16} \times 31\frac{1}{8}$ in. (65.9 × 79.3 cm.)

Acquired Paul Mellon Fund 1980
B1980.6

130. JAMES McNEILL WHISTLER (1834-1903)

The Adam and Eve, Old Chelsea, 1879

Etching in brown ink on laid paper
plate: $6\frac{15}{16} \times 11\frac{7}{8}$ in. (17.6 × 38.2 cm.)
sheet: $9\frac{13}{16} \times 15$ in. (24.9 × 38.2 cm.)
Signed with butterfly monogram within the plate mark

Gift of Mr and Mrs Donald Holden 1984
B1984.12.13

RARE BOOKS

When the rare book collections were received at the Yale Center for British Art, in repeated shipments that turned most of 1976 into an extended Christmas season, it was clear that they comprised a magnificent, double resource.

One aspect of the collection had a fame which preceded it: the splendid illustrated books, mostly of the eighteenth and early nineteenth centuries, with large coloured plates in aquatint and lithography, many of them from the collection of Major John Roland Abbey. Although almost any type of illustrated book might be found among them, the strengths were in the areas of topography, travel, architecture, and the decorative arts.

Less known, but equally important to the research rôle the collection was to play, were the large number of 'reference' books, a phrase encompassing some of the richest source material for the study of the fine arts in Britain from the seventeenth to the nineteenth centuries. Contemporary drawing manuals, books of recipes for pigments and other artists' materials, catalogues of private collections and auction sales, early histories of art and works on aesthetics, and accounts of specific pictures, all abounded.

Not surprisingly, the very first title purchased under the acquisitions programme initiated ten years ago fell into this 'reference' category. It was Richard Dagley's *Compendium of the theory and practice of drawing and painting*, 1822, a common type of recipe book used by artists. Throughout the years since then, securing books of instruction of this sort has been a continuing goal of the department. Finds have ranged from the earliest native English drawing manual, Henry Peacham's *The art of drawing with the pen*, 1607, through to the many amateurs' guides of the nineteenth century (exemplified here by B.W. Gilbert's *Treatise on the art of mezzotinto pencilling*, commended as an accomplishment fitted for 'the fair sex'), and it continues to be a fertile area for discovery of new works.

We have not neglected the category of illustrated book most characteristic of our holdings at the beginning, namely topographical volumes. These books share obvious affinities with the landscape paintings, drawings, and prints held in other departments of the Center. Both native English topography, as, for example, displayed by Samuel Lysons in *Etchings of views and antiquities in the county of Gloucestershire*, 1791, and foreign scenery as recorded even in an 1857 edition of the Bible with moving lithographs by David Roberts, are well represented. These books serve a dual purpose: their illustrations stand in their own right as images; and they also record the state of the landscape, often with greater accuracy than paintings, while their texts include relevant information about history, antiquities (which are frequently illustrated as well), geography, and customs of a region.

One of the most fruitful areas for acquisitions has been among the often ephemeral pamphlets which were issued to accompany temporary exhibitions of paintings in London in the late eighteenth and early nineteenth centuries. Catalogues of works on exhibit at Macklin's Gallery of Poets, for example, or skimpier tracts such as those issued by Benjamin Robert Haydon and John Martin in explanation of individual paintings, provide important documentation of the art world of the time, as do catalogues of auction sales and pamphlets commenting on the Royal Academy. A small number of manuscripts have also been acquired with this aim in mind: the accounts, for example, of the publisher John Nichols with the engraver Barak Longmate, who provided the plates for several of Nichols's publications, open a window on an area of commerce in art that has been little documented.

Although the majority of acquisitions by the Rare Book Department in the past decade have been by purchase from the learned and helpful world of antiquarian booksellers — many of whom are owed our gratitude for finding unusual items for us — we have also profited from generous gifts from collectors and friends. The current exhibition benefits from the presence of a very important work in the history of British illustration, Bowyer's edition of Hume's *History of England*, 1800-10, the gift to us of Mr and Mrs William R. Ginsberg. Our complete run of *Punch* came to us from the late Henry S. Morgan; a copy of the rare periodical *Blast* was presented to us by John Brealey on the occasion of a small exhibition on Vorticism. These and other gifts have enriched the collections. And, of course, all the items purchased directly by us have been made possible by the generosity of our original donor, Paul Mellon, who has added to his generosity the fun of letting us find things ourselves.

It is a commonplace in the world of antiquarian books for dealers and collectors to bemoan the state of the market: sources of books are said to be drying up, as more and more collections enter institutional libraries, never to reappear in commerce. The past decade of scouting out volumes for the Yale Center for British Art has not shown this to be true. While some well-known and highly sought titles are no longer available for purchase, others, less obvious, but no less important and useful to research, have instead drawn our attention. We look forward to continuing to build this research tool in the decades ahead.

Joan M. Friedman
Curator of Rare Books

I. General Illustration/Caricature

131. GEORGE MOUTARD WOODWARD (1760?-1809)
Gradation from a greenhorn to a blood.
London: William Holland, 1790.

Acquired 15th May 1978. Paul Mellon Fund

Shown: plate [3], 'A Jessamy'. Aquatint after Woodward.

132. JAMES GILLRAY (1757-1815)
La Rigenerazione dell'Olanda specchio a tutti i popoli rigenerati . . .
Venice: Giovanni Zatta di Antonio, 1799.

Acquired 26th November 1984. Paul Mellon Fund
Shown: plate 6, 'Il Comitato di commercio e navigazione'. Etching printed
 in red by Gillray after David Hess (1770-1843).

A satire on the French Revolution.

133. BIBLE, ENGLISH. AUTHORISED VERSION
*The New Testament embellished with engravings from pictures and
 designs by the most eminent English artists . . .*
London: for Thomas Macklin by Thomas Bensley, 1800.

Acquired 12th August 1981. Paul Mellon Fund

Shown: Rev. XIX: 11-12, 'The Vision of the White Horse'. Engraving by
 John Landseer (1769-1852) after Philippe Jacques de Loutherbourg
 (1740-1812).

The 'Macklin Bible', like Boydell's Shakespeare and Bowyer's History
 (see catalogue no.135) featured illustrations engraved after paintings
 specially commissioned for the work. See also catalogue no.157.

134. MARIA COSWAY (b. 1759)
Imitations in chalk.
London: R. Ackermann, 1800

Acquired 8th August 1979. Paul Mellon Fund

Shown: Pt. I, No. 5 [untitled]. Soft-ground etching by Maria Cosway
 after Richard Cosway (1740-1821). **(Fig.22)**.

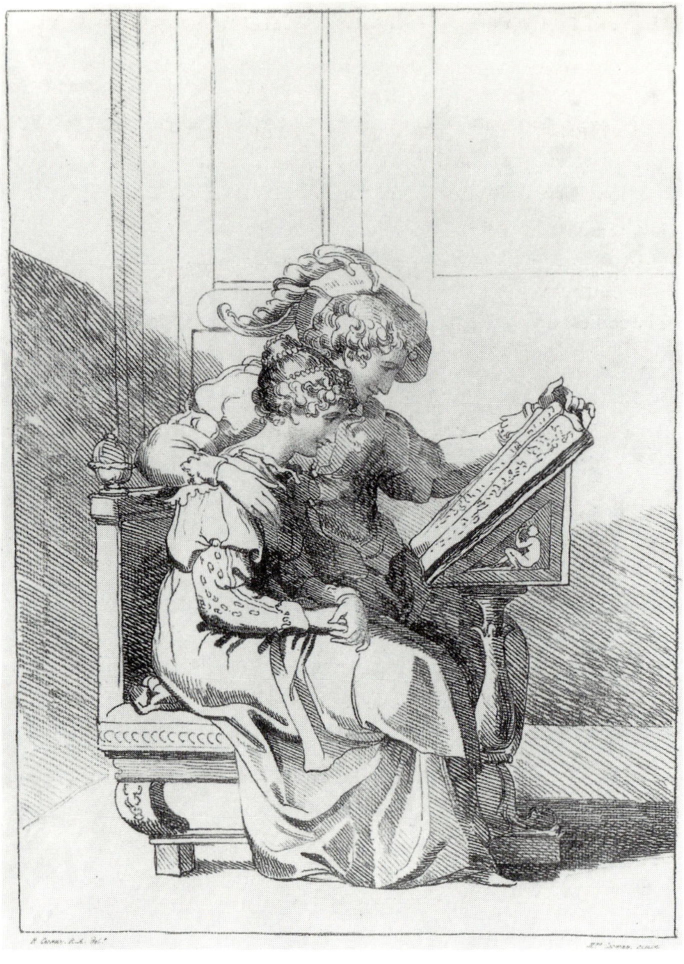

22. Maria Cosway, *Imitations in chalk*, CAT. 134

135. DAVID HUME (1711-1776)
History of England.
London: T. Bensley for Robert Bowyer, 1806.

Acquired 21st December 1979. Gift of Mr and Mrs William R. Ginsberg.

Shown: vol. 8, opp. p. 470, 'Charles I Taking Leave of His Children'.
 Engraving by William Bromley (1769-1842) after Thomas Stothard
 (1755-1834).

In addition to hoping to elevate the level of history painting in England
 by commissioning the paintings to illustrate this work, Bowyer aspired
 to finance the publication from admission fees to the gallery in which
 the paintings were exhibited.

136. JOHN WATKINS (fl. 1792-1831)
Boydell's heads of illustrious and celebrated persons.
London: W. Bulmer for Messrs. Boydell, 1811.

Acquired 15th November 1978. Paul Mellon Fund

Shown: opp. p. 61, 'Abrahamus Hondius Pictor'. Mezzotint by John
 Smith (1652?-1742) after Abraham Hondius (c. 1625-1695).

137. GEORGE GORDON NOEL BYRON, 6TH BARON BYRON
 (1788-1824)
Childe Harold's pilgrimmage. A romaunt.
London: John Murray, 1841.

Acquired 18th December 1980. Paul Mellon Fund

Shown: plate 13, 'The Acropolis'. Steel engraving by William Finden
 (1787-1852) after Henry Warren (1794-1879).
Presentation copy from John Murray to Edward Moxon.

138. *Punch, and London Charivari*
London: for the Proprietors, 1841.

Acquired 12th April 1980. Gift of Henry S. Morgan

Shown: vol. 1, p. 187, 'The New Parliamentary Masons'. Unsigned
 wood engraving.

139. HENRY SPENCER MOORE (1898-1986)
Heads, figures, and ideas.
London: George Rainbird, 1958.

Acquired 23rd October 1984. Paul Mellon Fund

Shown: [p. 43], 'UNESCO Group-Family'. Lithograph by Moore.

II. Art Instruction/Techniques/Anatomy

140. HENRY PEACHAM (1576?-1643?)
The art of drawing with the pen, and limming in water colours.
London: Richard Braddock for William Jones, 1607.

Acquired 23rd April 1979. Gift of Paul Mellon

Shown: pp.16-17 'Of drawing the face or countenaunce of a man'.
  Letterpress.

The earliest native English drawing manual first appeared as a section
  within a courtesy book.

141. GEORGE BICKHAM, JUNIOR (1706?-1771)
*General rules for painting in oil and water-colours; washing prints,
  maps, and mezzitintoes. With the whole art of japanning.*

London: for G. Bickham, 1747.

Acquired 16th May 1979. Paul Mellon Fund

Shown: pp.6-7. Letterpress.

142. GEORGE ALEXANDER STEVENS (1710-1784)
George Stevens' celebrated lecture on heads.
[London], [1766].

Acquired 4th September 1980. Paul Mellon Fund

Shown: 'Frontispiece to the Celebrated Lecture on Heads'. Unsigned
  etching.

Anatomy could be seen as a key to character.   **(Fig.23)**.

143. MARY GARTSIDE
*An essay on a new theory of colours, and on composition in general;
  illustrated by coloured blots shewing the application of the theory.*
London: J. Barfield for T. Gardiner, 1808.

Acquired 2nd October 1978. Paul Mellon Fund

Shown: opp. p.54, 'Application of the green blot, to a group of fern'.
  Unsigned water-colour.

144. CHARLES STANHOPE, 3RD EARL OF STANHOPE
  (1753-1816)
ALS to David Steuart Erskine, 11th Earl of Buchan (1742-1829).
Sevenoaks, 20th August 1812.

Acquired 31st October 1984. Paul Mellon Fund

Manuscript letter.

Stanhope speaks of a new process for producing large editions of prints,
  which will need new tools; probably refers to steel engraving.

145. *Rudiments of drawing, shadowing, and colouring flowers in
  water colours.*
London: H.K. Causton for G. Testolini, 1818 [i.e. 1817].

Acquired 9th May 1985. Paul Mellon Fund

Shown: Plate 10, 'Scarlet Horse Shoe Geranium'. Unsigned aquatint.

146. CHARLES LeBRUN (1619-1690); ed. J.P. Blanquet
*A series of lithographic drawings illustrative of the relation between
  the human physiognomy and that of the brute creation.*
London: James Carpenter, 1827.

Acquired 9th March 1982. Paul Mellon Fund

Shown: Plate 20 [horse]. Lithograph by Engelmann, Graf, Coindet after
  Eustache Hyacinthe Langlois (1777-1837).

LeBrun's 'anatomy of expression' has by this time evolved considerably;
  animal physiognomy is here seen as a clue to depicting human character.

147. B.W. GILBERT
A treatise on the art of mezzotinto pencilling.
London: for the Author, 1831.

Acquired 28th July 1981. Paul Mellon Fund

Shown: p.[1], 'Observations on mezzotinto pencilling'. Letterpress.

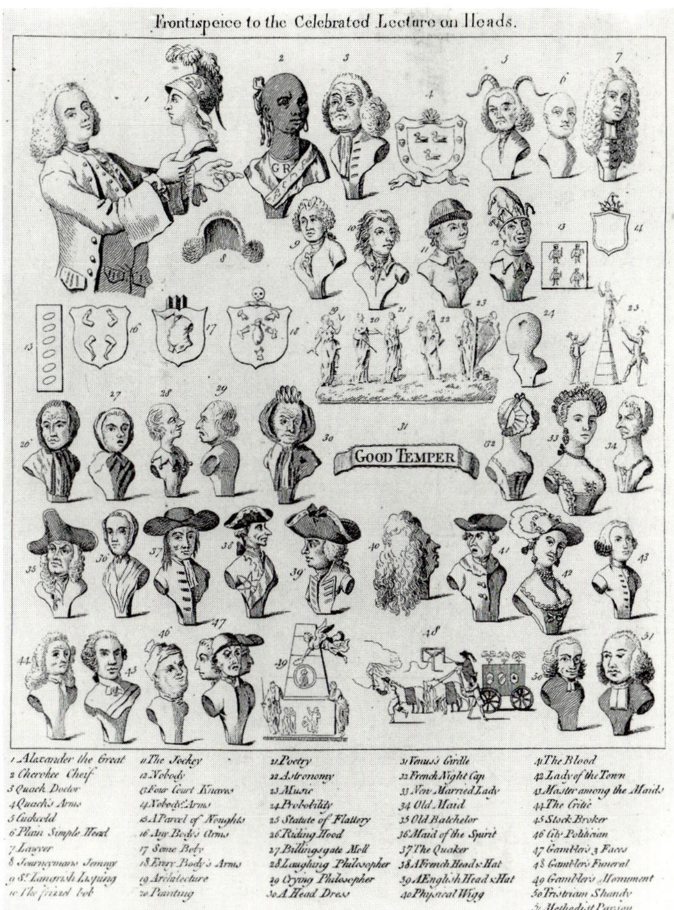

23. George Alexander Stevens, *George Stevens' celebrated lecture on heads*, CAT. 142

III. Art World Documentation

148. CESARE RIPA (fl.1600)
Iconologia; or, moral emblems.
London: Benj. Motte, 1709.

Acquired 2nd February 1979. Paul Mellon Fund

Shown: Plate 16, 'Confidence' 'Conjugal Love' 'Preservation' and 'Divine & Humane things Joyn'd'. Etching by Pierce Tempest (1653-1717).

149. JOHN NICHOLS (1745-1826)
MS accounts with the engraver Barak Longmate (1768-1836).
London, 1807-1815.

Acquired 23rd October 1984. Paul Mellon Fund

Shown: [f.4], 'Mr Nichols An Account of Leicestershire B. Longmate'. Manuscript.

The accounts recording what Longmate charged for providing the illustrations, head- and tail-pieces for *The History of Leicestershire*. He includes his incidental expenses in the reckoning.

150. JAMES BARRY (1741-1806)
Lectures delivered in the Royal Academy.
London: T. Cadell and W. Davies, 1811.

Acquired 24th October 1979. Paul Mellon Fund

Shown: Front cover inscribed: 'Presented to Mr. Daniel McClise [sic] for the best copy made in the painting school, Royal Academy of Arts. London. December X. MDCCCXXX'. Stamped calf binding.

151. ROBERT HARDING EVANS (1778-1857)
A catalogue of more than five thousand copper plates, engraved by the most esteemed British artists.
London: Evans, 1818.

Acquired 7th July 1986. Paul Mellon Fund

Shown: p.5. Letterpress.

Auction sale of the Boydells' stock after their death; interleaved and annotated with prices and buyers. Running total at the end shows a total of £23,788-0-6 realized in the sale.

152. 'A.E.' i.e. RICHARD JAMES LANE (1800-1872)
Marks and re-marks for the catalogue of the exhibition of the Royal Academy.
London: W.J. Colbourn, 1856.

Acquired 9th April 1980. Paul Mellon Fund

Shown: pp.16-17. Letterpress.

153. JOHN MURRAY (1778-1843)
Mr. Murray's illustrated list of works.
London: John Murray, 1856.

Acquired 23rd June 1986. Paul Mellon Fund

Shown: [p.17], announcement of *A Handbook For Young Painters*. Letterpress and wood engraving after Adrian van Ostade (1610-1685).

154. SIR EDWARD COLEY BURNE-JONES (1833-1898)
ALS to John Ruskin (1819-1900).
The Grange, West Kensington, [1887].

Acquired 24th January 1980. Paul Mellon Fund

Manuscript letter.

Remarks to Ruskin upon receiving the new volume of *Praeterita*; addressed 'Ho blessed one'.

155. WYNDHAM LEWIS (1882-1957)
Blast, no. 2 'War Number'.
London, 1915.

Acquired 11th January 1983. Gift of John Brealey

Shown: p.63, 'Design for "Red Duet"'. Woodcut by Lewis.

IV. Exhibition Catalogues

156. JAMES BARRY (1741-1806)
An account of a series of pictures in the Great Room of the Society of Arts, Manufactures, and Commerce, at the Adelphi.
London: William Adlard for T. Cadell, 1783.

Acquired 20th March 1978. Paul Mellon Fund

Shown: p.59, 'Fourth Picture. Commerce, or the Triumph of the Thames'. Letterpress.

157. THOMAS MACKLIN
Catalogue of the third exhibition of pictures, painted for Mr. Macklin by the artists of Britain, illustrative of the British poets, and the Bible.
London: T. Bensley, 1790.

Acquired 16th November 1982. Paul Mellon Fund

Shown: pp.38-39, 'Proposals for Macklin's Bible'. Letterpress.

158. JACQUES-LOUIS DAVID (1748-1825)
Le tableau des sabines exposé publiquement au Palais national . . .
Paris: P. Didot, 1800.

Acquired 28th June 1984. Paul Mellon Fund

Shown: p.2. Letterpress.

David justified exhibiting this picture by comparing it to Benjamin West's *Death of Chatham* and *Death of Wolfe*.

159. BENJAMIN WEST (1738-1820)
The Gallery of pictures painted by Benjamin West Esqr.
London, 1811.

Acquired 12th January 1981. Paul Mellon Fund

Shown: Plate IV, 'The Captive'. Etching by Henry Moses (1782?-1870) after Henry Corbould (1787-1844), after West.

160. ROBERT BURFORD (1791-1861)
Description of a view of the city of New York, now exhibiting at the Panorama, Leicester Square.
London: T. Brettell, 1834.

Acquired 29th April 1986. Paul Mellon Fund

Shown: Frontispiece. Unsigned wood engraving.

Bound in a volume with twenty other similar pamphlets describing panoramic pictures Burford exhibited, 1826-48.

161. BENJAMIN ROBERT HAYDON (1786-1846)
Description of Haydon's picture of the great meeting of delegates held at the Freemason's Tavern . . . for the purpose of abolishing slavery . . . now exhibiting at the Egyptian Hall, Piccadilly.
London: Charles Reynell, 1841.

Acquired 19th February 1980. Paul Mellon Fund

Shown: pp. 12-13. Letterpress.

Apparently author's proof copy with passages marked for deletion.

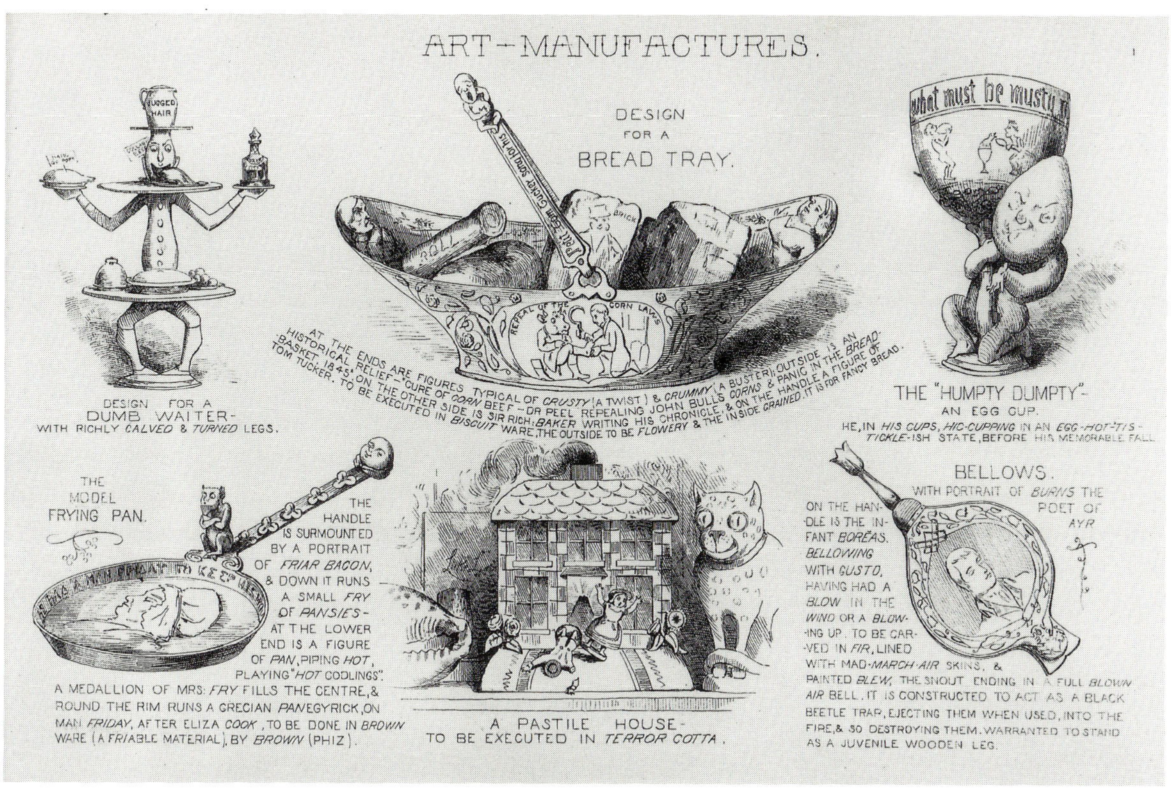

24. John Leighton, *Comic art-manufactures*, CAT. 163

25. A. W. N. Pugin, *Floriated ornament*, CAT. 164

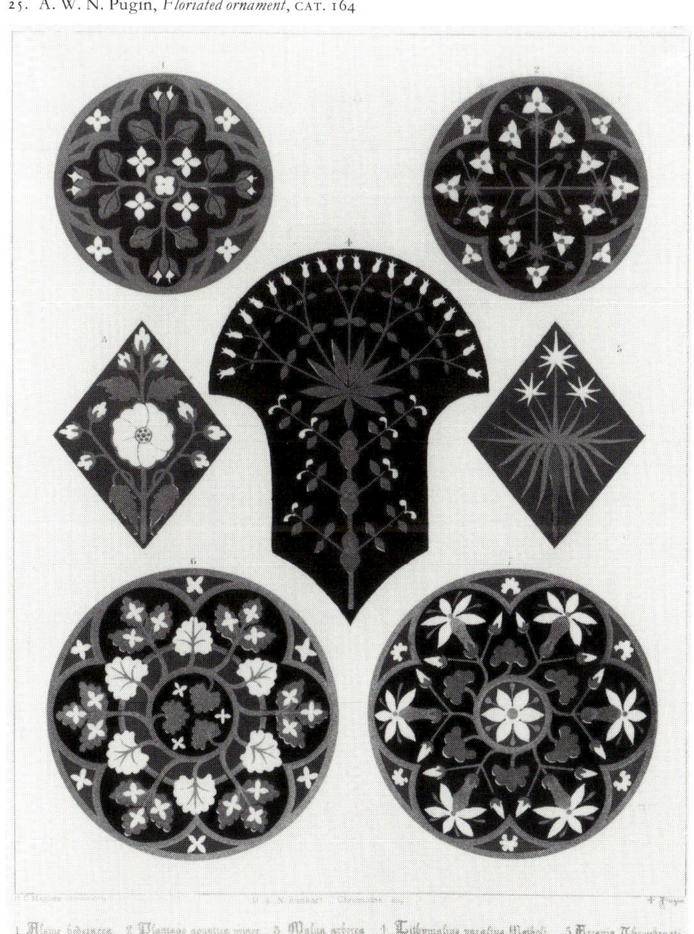

V. Decorative Arts

162. HENRY SHAW (1800-1873)

The encyclopedia of ornament.

London: William Pickering, 1842

Acquired 11th October 1983. Paul Mellon Fund

Shown: Plate 58, 'Painted Tiles from the Chapter House, Westminster'. Chromoxylograph by Shaw.

163. JOHN LEIGHTON (1822-1912)

Comic art-manufactures.

London: D. Bogue, 1848.

Acquired 9th April 1983. Paul Mellon Fund

Shown: p.1, 'Design for a Bread Tray' *et al.* Lithograph by Leighton.

A satire on Henry Cole's efforts to encourage 'art manufactures'. **(Fig.24)**

164. AUGUSTUS WELBY NORTHMORE PUGIN (1812-1852)

Floriated ornament.

London, 1849.

Acquired 13th October 1980. Paul Mellon Fund

Shown: Plate 29: 'Fleine hederacea . . .' Chromolithograph by H.C. Maguire after Pugin. **(Fig.25)**.

165. *Journal of Design and Manufactures.*

London, 1850.

Acquired 9th April 1980. Paul Mellon Fund

Shown: vol.III, no.14 (April 1850), bet. pp.64 & 65: 'Calico'. Fabric samples and letterpress.

166. FREDERICK EDWARD HULME (1841-1909)

Suggestions in floral design.

London: Cassell Petter & Galpin, [1878-79].

Acquired 10th May 1979. Paul Mellon Fund

Shown: Plate XIV, [Primrose and Fern]. Chromolithograph by Dupuy & Fils after Hulme.

VI. Colour Printing

167. VIRGIL; ED. JOHN MARTYN (1699-1768)
The Georgicks of Virgil.
London: Richard Reily for the Editor, 1741.

Acquired 7th April 1978. Paul Mellon Fund

Shown: opp. p.353, 'Hiacinthus Poeticus'. Unsigned colour mezzotint.

168. GEORGE ALEXANDER HOSKINS (d.1864)
Travels in Ethiopia above the second cataract of the Nile.
London: Longman, Rees, Orme, Brown, Green, & Longman, 1835.

Acquired 24th May 1985. Paul Mellon Fund

Shown: after p.328, 'Grand Procession. Part I'. Chromolithograph by
Charles Joseph Hullmandel (1789-1850) after Hoskins.

Earliest English chromolithograph, printed by Charles Hullmandel;
first state, with black caps coloured by hand.

169. JOSEPH WATERHOUSE
*Vah-Ta-Ah, the Feejeean Princess: with occasional allusions to
Feejeean customs; and illustrations of Feejeean life.*
London: Hamilton, Adams and Co., 1857.

Acquired 28th October 1980. Paul Mellon Fund

Shown: Frontispiece, 'Vah-Ta-Ah, The Feejeean Princess'.
Chromoxylograph by George Baxter (1804-1867) after J.D. Macdonald.

170. JAMES WILLIAM EDWARD DOYLE (1822-1892)
A Chronicle of England B.C.55-A.D.1485.
London: Longman, Green, Longman, Roberts & Green, 1864.

Acquired 18th August 1978. Paul Mellon Fund

Shown: p.293: 'Mortimer seized by the king'. Chromoxylograph by
Edmund Evans (1826-1905) after Doyle.

171. J.M. KRONHEIM
Colour & progressive sheets.
London, 1869.

Acquired 22nd July 1983. Paul Mellon Fund

Shown: Plate [8]: 'Dignity' [4 tint blocks only]. Chromoxylograph by
Kronheim & Co. after Charles Green (1840-1898).

Progressive proofs of a plate included in L.J. Valentine's *The nobility of
life*, 1869.

VII. Travel/Topography

172. SAMUEL LYSONS (1763-1819)
Etchings of views and antiquities in the county of Gloucestershire.
London: A. Strahan for T. Cadell, [1791].

Acquired 7th April 1980. Paul Mellon Fund

Shown: Plate XLII, 'The Market-Place at Cirencester'. Unsigned etching.

Volume is publisher's proof, assembled about ten years before the title
was published; several plates are marked for deletion.

173. JAMES HAKEWILL (1778-1843)
Series of views of the neighbourhood of Windsor.
London: for B.E. Lloyd and Son, 1820.

Acquired 22nd March 1979. Paul Mellon Fund

Shown: opp. p.4, 'South West View of Windsor Castle'. Etching by
Letitia Byrne (1779-1849) after Hakewill.   **(Fig.26)**.

174. H. HASELER
A series of views of Sidmouth and its neighbourhood.
Sidmouth: H. Haseler, 1825.

Acquired 22nd June 1986. Paul Mellon Fund

Shown: Plate [2], 'View taken from the grotto in Mr. Fish's garden
Sidmouth'. Lithograph by Charles Joseph Hullmandel (1789-1850)
after Haseler.

Early unrecorded lithographic product from Hullmandel.

175. FRANCIS NICHOLSON (1753-1844)
Views in the Tyrol.
London: The Lithographic Establishment, 1828.

Acquired August 1981. Paul Mellon Fund

Shown: Plate [10], 'The Gorge in the Calvario Mountain, Near Zils'.
Lithograph by Nicholson after the Hon. Mrs. Fortescue.

176. SIR CHARLES D'OYLY, 7TH BART. (1781-1845)
Costumes of India.
Behar: The Lithographic Press, 1830.

Acquired 8th August 1979. Paul Mellon Fund

Shown: Plate [4], 'Fishers of Small Fry'. Hand-coloured lithograph by
D'Oyly after George Chinnery (1748-1847).

177. JAMES DUFFIELD HARDING (1798-1863)
Illustrations of the Book of Exodus.
London: Henry Colburn and Richard Bentley, 1830.

Acquired 13th August 1985. Paul Mellon Fund

Shown: Plate II, 'The Convent at Mount Sinai'. Lithograph by Harding
after William H. Newnham.

The topographical illustrations of this volume depict the contemporary
Near East rather than the Biblical scenes the title implies.

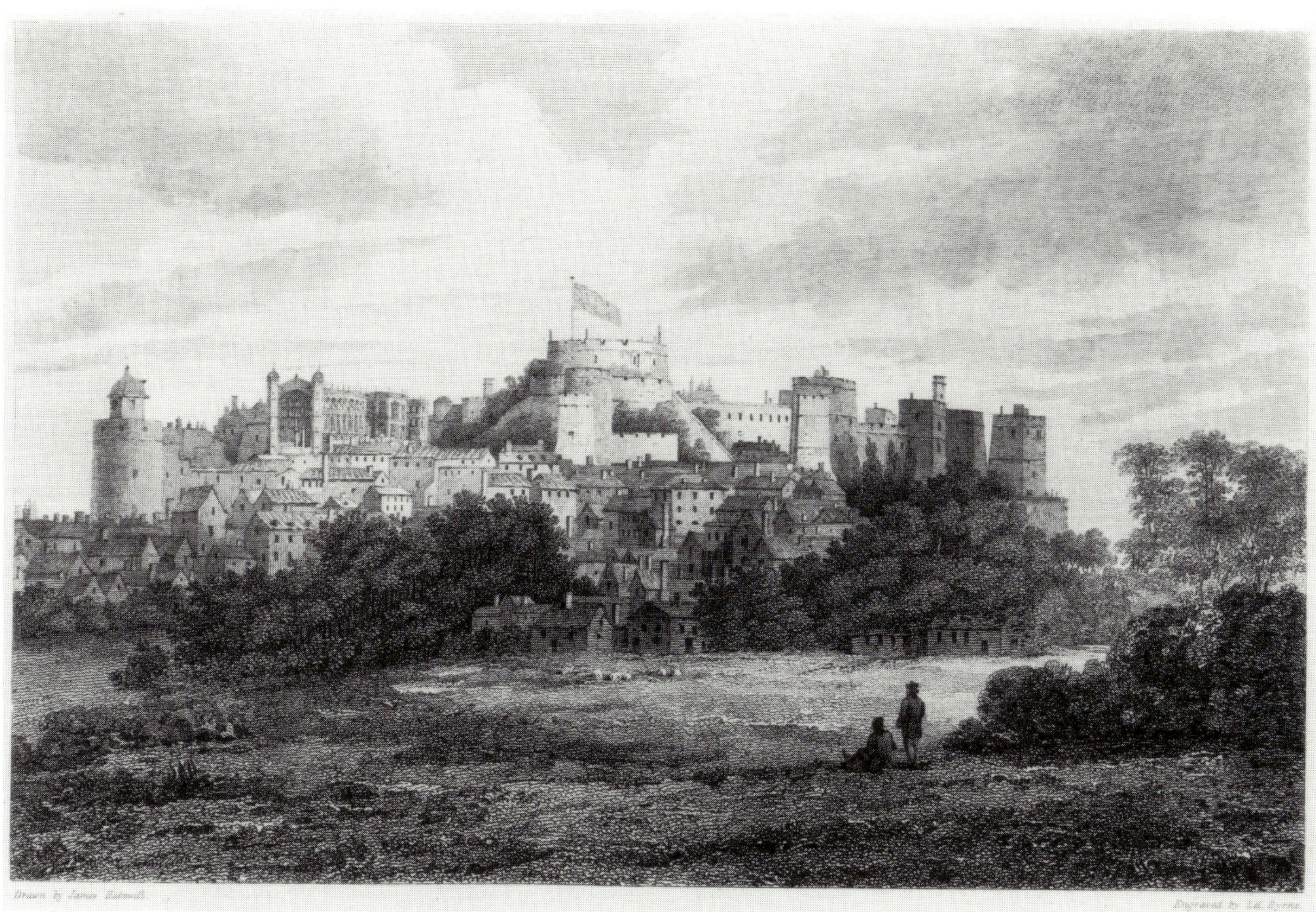

26. James Hakewill, *Series of views in the neighbourhood of Windsor*, CAT.173

178. SIR HENRY MANGLES DENHAM (1800-1887)

*Sailing directions from Point Lynas to Liverpool . . . for navigating
    the Dee and Mersey.*

Liverpool, 1840.

Acquired 16th June 1986. Paul Mellon Fund

Shown: Plate M: 'Appearance of the Cheshire shore of the Mersey'.
    Unsigned lithograph.

179. BIBLE. ENGLISH. AUTHORISED VERSION

*The Holy Bible, according to the Authorised Version . . . with
    maps and tinted landscapes, illustrative of the lands of the Bible.*

London and Glasgow: Richard Griffin, 1857.

Acquired 23rd April 1980. Paul Mellon Fund

Shown: opp. p.860, 'Petra, showing the upper or eastern end of the
    valley'. Tinted lithograph by Day & Son after David Roberts
    (1796-1864).

This catalogue was first published in the October 1986 issue of
The Burlington Magazine

It accompanies an exhibition at the
Yale Center for British Art, New Haven, Connecticut
19 November 1986 – 25 January 1987

Cover illustration: catalogue number 42

Photography by Michael Marsland and Joseph Szaszfai

Copyright © 1986 Burlington Magazine Publications Ltd
and the Yale Center for British Art

Library of Congress Catalogue Card Number 86–05 1189
ISBN 0–930606–54–X

Designed by The Burlington Magazine
Typeset and printed in Great Britain by Jolly & Barber Limited, Rugby